The Observers Series
INSECTS OF THE BRITISH ISLES

About the Book

This is a pocket guide to all the twenty-five orders of insects found in the British Isles. It uses up-to-date classification methods as accepted today and includes a useful key to all the British insect orders. A comprehensive account of the orders is given in the text and there are numerous colour illustrations, photographs and line drawings. Great care has been devoted to the colour illustrations. A section on spiders is included because of the interrelationship between them and the insects.

E. F. Linssen had the happy ability of presenting facts of a vast subject in a concise yet comprehensive manner that gives the reader a clear picture of the whole of the range of our British insects.

This revised edition of the book has been prepared for the publishers by John Clegg, the author of *Observers Pond Life*.

About the Author

E. F. Linssen was a Scientific Fellow of the Zoological Society and a Fellow of the Royal Entomological Society. His main interests were microscopy and the study of the smaller species of animal and plant life. He was a well-known and enthusiastic photographer of these subjects, on which he wrote a number of books. These include two volumes (published by Warne): *Beetles of the British Isles* and *The Observer's Book of Common Insects and Spiders*, the latter being replaced by the present book.

He also edited various books and published work on microscopy, stereoscopy, photography, entomology and on the graphic arts. He edited the English edition of the well-known international photographic journal, *Leica Fotografie*. E. F. Linssen travelled extensively in pursuit of his various interests.

The *Observer's* series was launched in 1937 with the publication of *The Observer's Book of Birds*. Now, almost sixty years on, the series still provides practical, useful information on a wide range of subjects, and with every book regularly revised by experts, the facts are right up-to-date. Students, amateur enthusiasts and professional organisations alike will find the latest *Observers* invaluable.

'Thick and glossy, briskly informative' – *The Guardian*

'If you are a serious spotter of any of the things the series deals with, the books must be indispensable' – *The Times Educational Supplement*

O B S E R V E R S

INSECTS

OF THE BRITISH ISLES

with a section on Spiders

E. F. Linssen F.Z.S., F.R.E.S.

CLAREMONT BOOKS

PENGUIN BOOKS

Published by the Penguin Group
Penguin Books Ltd, 27 Wrights Lane, London W8 5TZ, England
Penguin Books USA Inc., 375 Hudson Street, New York, New York 10014, USA
Penguin Books Australia Ltd, Ringwood, Victoria, Australia
Penguin Books Canada Ltd, 10 Alcorn Avenue, Toronto, Ontario, Canada
M4V 3B2
Penguin Books (NZ) Ltd, 182–190 Wairau Road, Auckland 10, New Zealand

Penguin Books Ltd, Registered Offices: Harmondsworth, Middlesex, England

This edition first published in Great Britain in 1953 by
Frederick Warne

This revised edition published in 1996 by Claremont Books,
an imprint of Godfrey Cave Associates Limited,
42 Bloomsbury Street, London WC1B 3QJ

Copyright © Frederick Warne & Co., 1953, 1978, 1987
All rights reserved

ISBN 1 85471 048 6

Printed in Italy

CONTENTS

Illustrations Note
Sizes of insects vary a good deal and the magnification is a
rough guide to the average size of the insect.

PREFACE

EVERY INSECT order found in the British Isles is outlined in this pocket-book, and illustrations are given of many of the more common species. No book can, however, in any manner deal adequately with the whole of our insect fauna, of which we have over 25,000 species, and consequently writers can give only a generalized picture of insects made up from a few selected examples of common species.

Because of the dependence of spiders on insects for food, and in deference to a custom of including them in popular books, they have been included in this volume—notwithstanding the fact that they belong to an entirely separate class of animals.

All the photographs reproduced in this book are by the author, with the exception of those numbered 102–3, which are by E. Botting, and 184, by S. C. Bisserot. The drawings are by Gordon Riley, who also acknowledges the help of Janet Dawson and John Crocker.

The publishers wish to record their appreciation of Mr. Linssen's friendly interest and co-operation at all times throughout their long association with him. It is a matter of sorrow that after completing his text he did not live to see its publication.

The publishers are grateful to Mr. John Clegg for preparing this revised edition of Mr. Linssen's book, and to Mr. Brian Hargreaves for supplying approximate magnifications of the insect diagrams.

INTRODUCTION

It is not known how many species of insects there are in the world. Over a million have been scientifically described and estimates of the total number range from 3.5 to 30 million. Even in well-worked Britain, each year there are new local records. There are at least eight insect species to every one of all other animals put together, and there are over 25,000 kinds of British insects, a most respectable number for islands having a mild temperature climate. The number of insect species thus outnumbers in a most prodigious manner every other kind of life known, whether it be animal or plant.

Insects are to be found everywhere. They live on plants and animals, or inside them. They are to be found in the air, in the earth, and in water. Some of them are as small as one-celled microscopical protozoa, and others are larger than some vertebrates. In the struggle for food they are man's undoubted and constant rivals, and they would defeat his proud dominion on earth were it not that they themselves are held in check by predators and parasites of their own kind. Only they themselves could do this. Darwin himself was appalled at times at the thought of 'the dreadful but quiet war of organic beings going on in the peaceful woods and fields'.

As to the number of individuals—this is evidently an impossible thing to guess at, but even so the latest estimate, using highly evolved scientific methods, gives the present population of one hectare of certain farmland in England as something like two thousand million! An equal number of mites (of the class Arachnida) was found to be present too!

What strikes us most about insects must surely be their energy, especially the persistence with which they apply it; nothing like this is to be found anywhere else in the animal kingdom. The pestering fly in sunshine and the blood-seeking mosquito at night are examples known to us all. The industry of the ant and the bee is another form of it, but in this instance man's admiration is aroused, and renowned philosophical writers like Maeterlinck derived inspiration from examples of virtues to be found among insects. Untiring labour, care of progeny, foresight, fidelity to the community, and the supreme self-sacrifice of the individual for the common good, are indeed qualities which we see exercised by many insects, especially by most bees, wasps, ants and, in warmer climates, termites. But to the entomologist of today such persistence of energy seems all too intimately bound up with an inability to profit from experience. Insects do not learn; they have no individuality. We need but know the peculiarities of a species to predict how its members will react to given conditions.

The behaviour of insects is governed by instinct. In the British Isles this may be seen developed in its highest form in ants, bees and wasps. Behaviour due to instinct is not learned, but is an inherited capacity, although it may be improved by practice.

8

The mysterious force of instinct is shown by the classic example of the hive bee, which on leaving the hive for the first time performs all the duties of an expert forager, as if it were a routine performance already done on numerous occasions. Strict routine behaviour is, however, peculiar to instinct, and is always associated with definite situations and occurrences at critical stages of an insect's life, as, for example, when the moment of pupation arrives, or when a dragonfly nymph climbs out of the water for the first time in its life in order that the fully developed dragonfly will be able to emerge in its own element, air, which is entirely foreign to the earlier stages of its life.

The quality of our thoughts and actions is due to our acquired experience and the processes of our brain. An insect has a brain, but it is not a true centralized nerve-centre, as in the higher animals. An insect's nervous system consists of a double cord of nerve running along the whole lower length of the body. There are swellings (*ganglia*) at intervals, from which branches of nerves lead into the body-segments. These ganglia have much independence of function and can act as local brains. It is significant that those which command important parts of the body are correspondingly larger in size; for instance, the thorax bears the legs and wings, and its ganglia are larger than those of the abdomen.

Facts such as these have therefore to be borne in mind when we would advance explanations based on analogy between our own behaviour and what causes it, and the phenomena of a similar kind which we may observe in insects. Such interpretations could easily lead us into complete error. However, although an insect is the puppet of the all-powerful instinct that dominates its life, this does not necessarily make it a mere automaton. If an insect is driven on by instinct and energy, we shall nevertheless perceive that occasionally there is present an awareness of situations, especially in the more evolved species, which indicates some vague mental process which is able to exercise some learning, judgement and control.

It is interesting at this stage, before proceeding further, to compare the conclusions of a present-day naturalist, R. W. G. Hingston, with the reflections of another, the poet Brooke, written at the beginning of the last century. "Every animal, Man included, possesses two sets of mental activity: the one instinctive, automatic, innate; the other intelligent, plastic and acquired. These two activities are always blended. They may differ immensely in degrees of development, but they never completely separate from each other. The insect mind and the human mind differ mainly in the development of these two factors. . . . The insect, though predominantly instinctive, possesses also glimmerings of reason."* The poet tells of the structural wonders found in insects, and he does this in a way that is becoming all too rare:

Though numberless these insect tribes of air,
Though numberless each tribe and species fair,
Who wing the noon, and brighten in the blaze,
Innumerous as the sands which bend the seas;

* From *Problems of Instinct and Intelligence*, by R. W. G. Hingston (Edward Arnold & Co.).

These have their organs, arts, and arms, and tools,
And functions exercised by various rules;
The saw, the augur, trowel, piercer, drill;
The neat alembic, and nectareous still:
Their peaceful hours the loom and distaff know:
But war, the force and fury of the foe,
The spear, the falchion, and the martial mail,
And artful stratagem, where strength may fail,
Each tribe peculiar occupations claim,
Peculiar beauties deck each wavering frame.

Neither of these authors exaggerates what may be observed and studied in insects.

EXTERNAL STRUCTURE

When we look at an insect, say a beetle, we first notice its hard, characteristic 'skin'. This is composed of *chitin*, and forms a shell or case of armour-plating, at the same time fulfilling the important function of a skeleton—an external one, hence called an *exoskeleton*. All muscles are attached to the exoskeleton and support the internal organs of the insect, which are soft. A 'set' museum or cabinet specimen is hollow, everything within having dried up. The chitin of the exoskeleton is one of the most effectual of time-resisting materials known, and its indestructible nature, and the forms and colours with which it may be associated, are what have made entomology so particularly fascinating to collectors. This is especially so because it permits the arranging of attractive and permanent collections, which at the same time can be directly correlated with the enthralling life-histories of the insects and details of their behaviour.

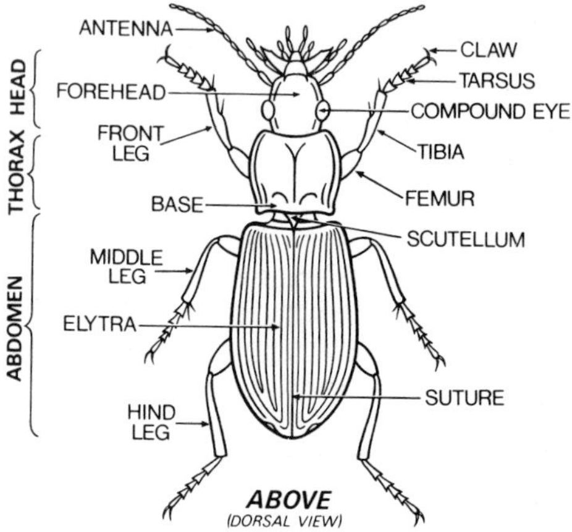
ANTENNA
CLAW
TARSUS
FOREHEAD
COMPOUND EYE
HEAD
THORAX
FRONT LEG
TIBIA
BASE
FEMUR
SCUTELLUM
MIDDLE LEG
ABDOMEN
ELYTRA
SUTURE
HIND LEG
ABOVE
(DORSAL VIEW)

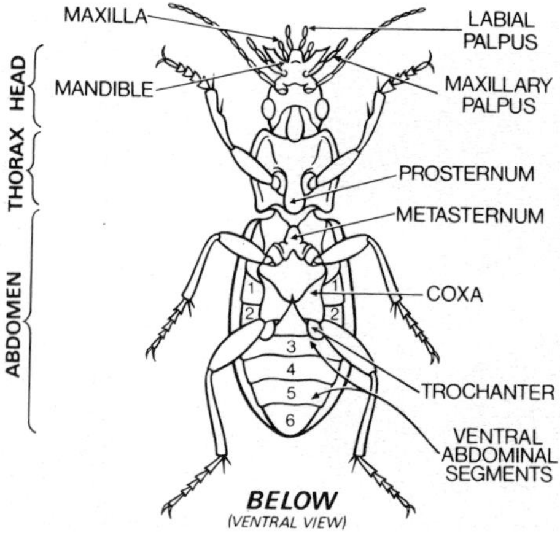
MAXILLA
LABIAL PALPUS
MANDIBLE
MAXILLARY PALPUS
HEAD
THORAX
PROSTERNUM
METASTERNUM
ABDOMEN
COXA
1
2
3
4
5
6
TROCHANTER
VENTRAL ABDOMINAL SEGMENTS
BELOW
(VENTRAL VIEW)

1 External structure of an insect

The nature of the exoskeleton and the method of breathing put a limit on the maximum size attainable by insects, but even so some exotic species of the order Orthoptera exceed 260 mm ($10\frac{1}{4}$ in) in length. Our largest native species are from the order Coleoptera—the Great Silver Water-beetle, *Hydrophilus piceus*, which attains a body length of 48 mm ($1\frac{7}{8}$ in) and the Stag Beetle, *Lucanus cervus*, which may attain 50 mm (2 in), while the Emperor Dragonfly, *Anax imperator*, among the order Odonata, achieves 75 mm (3 in) in length.

The class Insecta is sometimes called the Hexapoda (the six-legged), indicating an anatomical characteristic not found in other jointed, limbed animals. An insect's body has three divisions (1) the

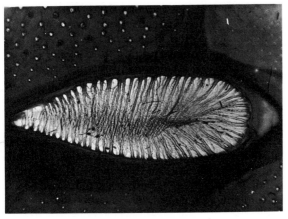

2 A spiracle

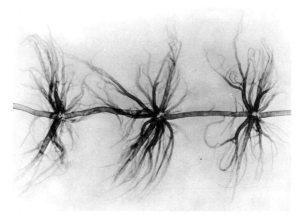

3 Tracheae (highly enlarged)

head, thorax (chest) and **abdomen.** The head
bears one pair of antennae (feelers or horns), which
are sensory in function. The mouth-parts are
complicated in structure and vary much in the
different insect orders, and also frequently at different periods of an insect's life. The thorax bears
the legs, and usually one or two pairs of wings.
Insects breathe through openings in the body (the
spiracles or *stigmata*, **2**) connected with an intricate
system of air-tubes (the *tracheae*, **3**). Most insects
undergo *metamorphosis* (transformation, *see* **4**) from
ovum (plural, *ova*: eggs), through *larva* (plural,
larvae: maggots, gentles, grubs, caterpillars) and
pupa (plural, *pupae*: chrysalids) to *imago* (plural,
imagines: adults).

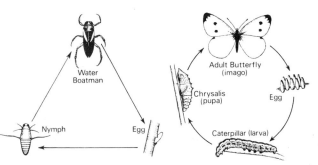

4 Some orders of insects undergo an incomplete metamorphosis, omitting the pupal stage as shown in the left diagram. A complete metamorphosis is illustrated on the right

THE EYES OF INSECTS

Insects have two kinds of eyes (**5,6**): *compound eyes* and *simple eyes* (or *ocelli*). One type may be present in an insect, or both, and many larvae have none.

The Simple Eye, or *ocellus*, is especially found in larvae, and not necessarily later in the adult insect (imago), but if present it is situated on the head between the **compound eyes**.

The Compound Eyes, restricted to one pair of eyes, are never found in larvae. They possess numerous facets. The house fly has about 4,000 facets, some dragonflies have as many as 28,000. Each facet helps to form a lens, which produces an image, and although no perfect picture of surroundings can be obtained, as can be obtained with our eyes, the compound eye is nevertheless eminently efficient for perceiving movements of near objects. The eye is also sensitive to certain colours.

The simple eye is much less efficient. It gives

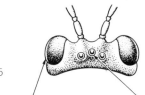

Compound eye   Simple eye or ocellus

5 Head of an insect with both types of eye (highly enlarged),
6 Structure of compound eye (highly enlarged).

only a rough image of near objects, its main function being to distinguish light from dark.

GLANDS

These organs, as in other creatures, are of extreme importance to insects. Glands produce secretions made from constituents drawn from the blood. In addition to the salivary and other glands, the following few may be noted, especially as they discharge their secretions out of the body, thus revealing their presence.

Wax Glands. A familiar example of the employment of wax is the use made of it by bees for making honeycomb. Wax glands are also present in some land bugs. The secretion which is discharged as 'honey-dew' by many aphids is the best known example after that of honeycomb.

Exuvial Glands are present in the larvae of some moths, sawflies and beetles, the secretion being used to help moulting. A further exudation with an analogous function is used by the Puss Moth, *Cerura vinula*, for softening a part of its very hard pupal case just before emergence.

Silk Glands are usually situated in the head, and are used by the larvae of many insects for forming cocoons. They occur in many species of butterflies and moths, including the important silkworms (species of moths) of commerce. Caterpillars are noteworthy in having silk glands which are modified salivary glands, saliva being provided by other glands. Many bees, wasps and ants use silk for cocoons, and caddis flies use it for constructing their cases.

Poison Glands. The secretions of these vary in their constituents. Poison is used for defence, paralysing or killing. In bees and wasps the venom injected with the sting is a complex mixture of proteins and other substances. Ants inject formic acid. The setae or 'hairs' of some caterpillars are brittle, and when broken discharge a liquid like a nettle-sting which can be very irritating to the skin.

Scent Glands. Secretions from these are discharged to attract the opposite sex, or their function may be to make the insect's presence acceptable to a totally different species. The larvae of many Lycaenidae (the butterfly family of Blues, Coppers and Hairstreaks) have an odour attractive to ants, who may be seen stroking a caterpillar's back, where the gland is situated, in order to obtain the secretion. Under this heading also may be mentioned the curious habit of *reflex-bleeding*. Some insects are able to eject blood from certain articulations; they do this when feigning death. Such blood contains repellants of the caustic kind which make the insects distasteful as food. Some of the bugs and members of the grasshopper and cricket family are able to do this, and the same habit is especially prevalent among several beetles such as members of the genera *Meloe*, *Cantharis*, *Coccinella* and *Timarcha* (pages 160–168). Some insects produce pheronomes. These are volatile substances which attract males so that mating can take place. An example of this, well known to collectors, is that of the Emperor Moth, *Pavonia pavonia*. A freshly emerged female in a box will allure a large number of males, and there is on record the capture of 11,000 males of a sawfly by the scent of one female.

CLIMATE AND WEATHER

The general influence of climate and the time of the year on plant and animal life needs no emphasis, though a specific example from the Insecta will indicate how delicate this can be; it also illustrates that our unpredictable weather exercises its power too. The Purple Emperor butterfly, *Apatura iris*, emerges in July in oak forests in the British Isles; the ruling factor is temperature which may not be less than 16°C (61°F), nor may the rainfall exceed 1066 mm (42 in); these are factors that exclude this butterfly from extending its range in the North and East of the country. If the limits mentioned are passed there will be no Purple Emperors.

THE PRODUCTION OF SOUND

The primary reason for the production of sound is either to attract attention or to serve as a warning to other individuals. The same reasons obtain among insects, though sound-production is often restricted to the males. Insects have no true voice, sound being made in various other ways: by *tapping* an object, by *vibrations* of various kinds, and by *friction* between different parts of the body.

The Death Watch Beetle taps its head against the floor. It does this especially from April to May, and the knocking is a sexual call. The buzzing of bees and beetles is in part due to the rapid vibrations of the wings. In flies sound-production is rather more complicated, and is the subject of several theories; certainly the rapid vibrations of the thorax, which is coupled with the wing-muscles, cause the rapid passage of air through the spiracles, providing one important method of sound-production.

Besides the cicadas, which have the most highly developed sound-producing apparatus of all insects—though we have only one very restricted species in the British Isles—the most interesting insects are our various grasshoppers. They produce sound by friction, known as *stridulation*, and this is the commonest method. It occurs especially in the orders of the grasshoppers, the true bugs and the beetles. It also happens in some ants and even in a few moths.

Among our grasshoppers stridulation is restricted to the males of short-horned and long-horned grasshoppers and crickets. Short-horned grasshoppers have a series of points on the hind legs, about eighty or ninety of them, which are rubbed against the hardened veins of the closed tegmina (wingcase-like fore wings). The action makes the tegmina vibrate to give a low buzzing sound. In the two other families, the long-horned grasshoppers and the crickets (Gryllidae), stridulation is effected by rubbing together two specially modified parts of the hardened fore wings.

Many beetles stridulate and for this purpose parts of the body are provided with a file-and-rasp mechanism.

COLORATION OF INSECTS

We are all attracted to colours, especially when several are to be seen in one object, where they may be blended harmoniously or stand out vividly in contrast to each other. The first sympathetic study of insects must have originated from interest awakened by species exhibiting attractive colour-patterns, particularly those seen in butterflies and beetles, many of which were depicted in the works of early artists. The zoologist of today does not, when considering the lower animals, refer to the colours they exhibit in terms of feelings evoked, and certainly not with regard to an insect's likes or dislikes regarding them, for we have seen the danger of explanations based on making comparisons with human reactions.

The Significance of Coloration. There has been much scientific discussion on the significance of insect coloration, and here we may state briefly that colours are not to be considered as necessarily due to some capricious act of nature. The coloration has many attributes, though it may mostly be divided roughly into warning coloration and concealing coloration. A warning coloration advertises the inedibility of an insect, such colours being black, white, yellow and red, and these colours may

7 Old Lady Moth, *Mormo maura* ×1

also be associated with aggressive insects, such as wasps. Many other insects derive protection from predators by exhibiting colour-patterns mimicking those of inedible or aggressive species. For example, the Wasp Beetle, *Clytus arietis* (**256, 265**) displays the colours of a redoubtable stinger; the beetle is quite harmless. Protective coloration, on the other hand, conceals the insect from detection. Examples here are the Old Lady Moth, *Mormo maura* (**7**) and the Lappet Moth, *Gastropacha quercifolia*.

The Nature of Insect Coloration. White light consists of many colours, and when these are separated from each other, they display the many hues seen in a rainbow. If any colours, say the reds, are removed from white light, we shall then see only those that remain, which in this instance will be greens. Green is said to be 'complementary' to red.

The presence of colour therefore signifies that white light has been interfered with and this may be on account of (i) *absorption* of part of the rays, the complementary rays being reflected, and only they being visible. The absorption is determined by the pigments present in the substance illuminated. Such colours are referred to as being 'pigmentary' or 'chemical'; (ii) *physical interference*, due to the structural nature of the surface illuminated. It gives rise to iridescent or 'metallic' colours, known to entomologists as 'structural colours'.

The two colour factors mentioned are frequently combined and are therefore referred to as 'combination colours'. Structural colours are seldom found alone, and when they are combined with the pigmentary kind they produce exceedingly beautiful effects.

The need for field study, as in every branch of natural history, applies just as much to that of the insect colours themselves. It is a mistake to imagine

8 Angle Shades Moth, *Phlogophora meticulosa* ×2

that the beautiful colours of a specimen as seen in a collector's cabinet necessarily possess the same richness and variety of hues to be seen in the living insect. For example, the attractive olive-green triangular markings of the Angle Shades moth, *Phlogophora meticulosa* (**8**), fade after death.

MASS BEHAVIOUR

There are times when insects abandon the normal routine of their lives. The local population of a species may be seen to become agitated as a whole and to leave their surroundings. They may migrate to distant lands impelled by some mysterious urge, or they may be compelled to seek other sites for reasons that can be explained. It is a fascinating subject for further study.

Migration. The remarkable fact that many insects migrate came as a great surprise to entomologists when they became aware of it. In the British Isles it was soon realized by collectors that several species of butterfly came from abroad, like the Painted Lady, *Cynthia cardui* (**112**), which comes to England from as far away as North Africa! The transition involves crossing two seas without any difficulty. Although this species is widely distributed in Europe and North America, there is a more spectacular example in North America, the Monarch butterfly, *Danaus plexippus*; its flights cover fantastic distances in incredible numbers.

While investigating entomologists were observing butterflies migrating across the Pyrenees they noted at the same time that many species of beetles were also crossing the mountains. Indeed not only butterflies migrate, many moths do so too, and certainly insects of other orders do likewise. The daylight fliers can at least be observed and flight paths followed with the aid of field glasses; at night this is obviously impossible but we may infer from sudden, rapid population changes that many species of moth also migrate. What other orders of insects have migrants? Migration occurs among such significant pests as aphids (a well known example being the Bean Aphid, *Aphis fabae*) and dragonflies; and much is now known of our British immigrant butterflies, which originated scientific enquiry here. Further reference to this is made under butterflies and moths, Lepidoptera. The reason for insect migration is not known.

Swarming is quite another matter. It does not evoke a mystery such as that which surrounds migration. Insects swarm when there is a 'population explosion' which may be caused by very favourable weather conditions giving rise to an over-abundance of their specific food supply. The absence of natural enemies may be another important factor. Or they may belong to a species that is gregarious at times and which overwinters (hibernates) in large groups. In some countries where the summer season is inhospitable because the summer heat makes life difficult or impossible, they gather and shelter, staying immobile in large numbers. (They are then said to aestivate). Such large groups at rest derive protection when exhibiting a warning coloration—for example the ladybird beetles (Coccinellidae); of this family some hibernate, and elsewhere there are others of this useful kind that aestivate. Many members of other orders are noted for swarming. In our islands there are spring-tails, mayflies, ants, psocids, and a dragonfly, *Libellula quadrimaculata* among others.

Dispersal. An example of this occurs when a pond dries up and insects such as water bugs (Heteroptera) must then seek other water habitats. This is sometimes referred to as migrating, but it is merely dispersal to a congenial neighbouring habitat, a pond, a canal or the like.

CLASSIFICATION AND NOMENCLATURE

The beginner in natural history study soon realizes how essential it is to understand classification and nomenclature, not only because their existence in the world of science fulfils an obvious need, but also because of the greater enjoyment he will then derive from his observations, giving him a clearer picture of the inter-relationship of all living things.

The popular vernacular names of a particular species of insect, or indeed of any animal or plant, may differ entirely as one passes from district to district, and certainly from country to country. An occasional insect visitor from America to the south of England is the large and beautiful Monarch butterfly, which is also known as the Milkweed. Some species may have as many as a dozen popular names, and the same names may be given to two entirely different species. More often than not there is no popular name, especially for the majority of insects. The two-name (binominal) system of nomenclature, introduced by Carl Linnaeus (1707–

1778) in 1753, ensures the accurate naming of species; it is international, and its aim is to avoid all confusion. Thus the Monarch butterfly is called *Danaus plexippus* Linnaeus. This last name is that of the author who first gave a scientific description of the species, in the present case, Linnaeus himself, and it may be added in full or in an abbreviated form. We can only guess at the small proportion of the insect population of the world that has been scientifically described. As we acquire a more complete picture of the Insecta, or other forms of animal and plant life, it may happen that a revision of some nomenclature and classification becomes necessary, often to the annoyance of naturalists, and especially of beginners, who may be unaware of the many implications connected with the need for such accuracy and the respect for the historical precedence of names*.

Scientific accuracy, therefore, renders it indispensable that a system of universal naming, as distinct from the common or popular names, shall be employed. The nomenclature of species is often in Latin, two names being allocated to each species. The first signifies the **genus** (plural genera; this is

* Scientific nomenclature is always liable to revision as knowledge of species increases. In the present book it has been deemed advisable to keep to the classification used in *A General Textbook of Entomology*, by A. D. Imms, and as subsequently revised by Professor O. W. Richards and R. C. Davies. This advanced work is the one most widely consulted and may be readily found in all natural history libraries. It constitutes a veritable foundation from which specialization may begin.

known as the generic name), and the second the **species** (this is known as the specific name). For example, the commonest of all insects, the House Fly, is known as *Musca domestica* (genus *Musca*, species *domestica*). It is only in respect of a species as a whole that two names are used. A three-name (trinominal) expression is used for varieties and races of species. The Human Louse exhibits slight physical modifications according to whether it lives on the body or in the hair of the head. They are not two distinct species, but two races of the same louse and known as *Pediculus humanus corporis* and *Pediculus humanus capitis* respectively. A second use of three names is in respect of insects in which there are alternating generations (as among gall-causing insects), the third name then describing the form or generation.

Binominal and trinominal expressions are only given to species, all other groupings for families, super-families, orders, sub-orders and so on, being named by one word only.

The name of a **family** is obtained by adding *idae* to the root of the genus serving as the type. So we have the family Muscidae. In the same manner the **sub-family** is formed by adding *inae* to the radical: Muscinae. Our House Fly *domestica* belongs to the genus *Musca*, which is included in the sub-family Muscinae, which forms part of the family Muscidae. This family forms part of the **sub-order** Brachycera, this being one of the large divisions of the **order** Diptera, or two-winged flies.

The orders, such as Diptera, Hymenoptera (ants,

bees, wasps, etc.), Coleoptera (beetles), are the first groupings into which the insect **class** is divided. The class Insecta, with its related classes of Arachnida, Crustacea, etc., comprise the **phylum** Arthropoda. The several phyla constitute the **Animal Kingdom**.

The Arthropoda is the most extensive of the great divisions or phyla into which the Animal Kingdom is divided, and comprises a large assembly of animals to which the insect class belongs, as well as crustaceans, millipedes, spiders and their allies, centipedes and so on. Arthropods have an external shell-like skeleton consisting of a variable number of segments to which are attached paired jointed appendages. The skin is covered with a non-living cuticle of chitin which has to be periodically moulted as the animals grow.

It may here be pointed out, however, that no student of animal interdependence (which is so marked in the life-histories of insects and spiders) can remain for long unaware of several members of other classes included in the phylum Arthropoda. A few of the species of this exceedingly large assembly of animals are common in all gardens, rivalling insects and spiders as being among the best-known dwellers in our surroundings. Among those frequently to be found are woodlice, one species of which is very well known—at least, by sight—and millipedes and centipedes.

These three types of Arthropoda belong to three distinct classes, the Crustacea, the Diplopoda and the Chilopoda. The following particulars give a brief summary only of the ways in which the classes differ from each other.

The Crustacea, the class to which the terrestrial woodlice belong, comprises mainly aquatic animals, very varied in structure, such as lobsters, crabs, crayfish, shrimps, etc. They have two pairs of antennae and at least five pairs of legs.

The Diplopoda, or millipedes, have two pairs of legs to each segment of the body, with the exception of the first three segments. Millipedes and centipedes appear from a cursory examination of their anatomy to be quite closely related, but in fact they are only very distant cousins.

The Chilopoda, or centipedes, have only one pair of legs to a segment. The first pair of legs is modified into poison claws. Although 'centipede' means 'hundred-footed', the number of legs varies from fifteen to one hundred and seventy-three pairs, according to the species. The classes of Diplopoda and Chilopoda have several other important differences which we need not investigate here; however, their seemingly close relationship is the reason why they are often referred to as Myriapoda, though this is merely a term of convenience.

Arthropod classification is based mostly on observation of morphological (structural) peculiarities of external anatomy, from consideration of which naturalists are able to form groupings of closely related species.

The class INSECTA is divided into two distinct sub-classes, the *APTERYGOTA*, small wingless insects having little or no metamorphosis, and the

PTERYGOTA, having wings and metamorphosis very varied.

The sub-class of winged insects is split into two divisions, according to whether the wings develop internally or externally. The divisions are respectively known as the *EXOPTERYGOTA* and the *ENDOPTERYGOTA*. The table on pages 31–32 shows how the various British insects are grouped.

ORDERS OF THE CLASS INSECTA

A glance at the English names in this tabulation shows how varied are the insects contained in the 25 orders represented in the British Isles. The following key, which is a simplified one but nevertheless helpful, shows differences that separate species into orders; it is based on the physical (morphological) appearance of insects:

KEY TO CLASSIFICATION

(Orders printed in CAPITALS, other major divisions in *CURSIVE CAPITALS*)

1. Imagines (mature adults)
      wingless—refer to No. 2
      with wings—refer to No. 12
2. Body: long and slender, approximately the same width throughout. Legs: long, slender and similar to each other. Head: small, antennae threadlike.
      PHASMIDA
      (Stick Insects) . . . . . p. 65
   Not as above—refer to No. 3

3. Abdomen: joined to thorax by slender 'waist'. Head: prominent, antennae elbowed.

HYMENOPTERA

FORMICOIDEA (Ants) .... p. 145
Abdomen: not as above.

Head: antennae not elbowed   refer to No. 4
4. Body: laterally compressed.
Legs: strong, adapted for leaping.

SIPHONAPTERA

(Fleas) .... p. 130
Not as above—refer to No. 5
5. Body: dorso-ventrally compressed—
refer to No. 6
Body: not compressed—refer to No. 8
6. Body: size minute, insects found on plants, usually covered with powdery or waxy coating, or scale-like. (Males sometimes with anterior wings.)

HEMIPTERA

COCCOIDEA,   (Scale Insects) ..... p. 75
Not as above—refer to No. 7
7. Found as external parasites on mammals and birds.

(a) Legs: tarsal claws minute. Head: large, square-shaped. Abdomen: elongate. Found mainly on birds.

MALLOPHAGA

(Biting Lice) ..... p. 73
(b) Legs: tarsal claws well developed. Head: elongate. Abdomen: ovoid. Found mainly on mammals.

SIPHUNCULATA

(Sucking Lice). ... p. 73

8. Body: ovoid. Abdomen: Very slight de-
marcation with thorax; with pair of
cornicles (horny protuberances) on 6th
segment. Head: sucking mouthparts.
Insects found on plants.

HEMIPTERA
APHIDOIDEA   (Aphids, Greenfly,
Not as above—refer to No. 9
9. Body: elongate, less than 2 mm long.
Head: no antennae, no compound eyes.
Legs: first pair held forwards giving insect
appearance of being four-legged.

PROTURA
Head: with antennae—refer to No. 10
10. Body: elongate. Head: antennae many-
segmented. Legs: equally developed.
(a) Abdomen: terminates with 3 tails.

THYSANURA
(b) Abdomen: terminates with 2 tails.

DIPLURA
Not as above—refer to No. 11
11. Head: antennae usually 4-segmented,
compound eyes absent. Abdomen: 6-seg-
mented, usually with 3 pairs of appendages, the last being a forked organ adapted for springing.

COLLEMBOLA
12. (a) One pair of membranous wings—
refer to No. 13

(b) Two pairs of wings—refer to No. 14

13. (a) Wings: front pair membranous, hind pair modified into halteres.

DIPTERA
(True flies) . . . . p. 120

(b) Wings: front pair modified into small clubs, hind pair large, fan-shaped.

STREPSIPTERA
(Stylopids) . . . . p. 171

14. Wings: front pair transformed into leathery or hard, opaque shell-like elytra (wing covers) which may or may not cover the whole of the abdomen; the 2nd pair of wings are membranous and are folded beneath the elytra. The elytra almost always meet to form a straight mid-dorsal suture (dividing line).

COLEOPTERA
(Beetles) . . . . p. 152

Not as above—refer to No. 15

15. Wings: both pairs membranous, covered with minute scales which are often brightly coloured.

LEPIDOPTERA
(Butterflies,
Moths) . . . . p. 95

Wings: membranous area not covered with scales, though sometimes with transparent or with but few scales or hairs—

refer to No. 16

16. (a) Wings: when present fore wings larger than hind pair, some with butterfly-like scales. Antennae 12 to 50-segmented. Size: minute insects.

(b) Wings: when present, very narrow and margined with long hairs. Size: minute insects. Antennae 6 to 10-segmented.

Not as above—refer to No. 17

17. Wings: hind pair small and connected to fore pair by minute hooks.

Not as above—refer to No. 18

18. Wings: both pairs similar, front wings with texture uniform throughout, either horny or all membranous. Body: slender. Head: elongate with beak-like biting mouthparts; antennae long, filiform. Legs: long and slender. Abdomen: elongate with short 'tails'.

Not as above—refer to No. 19

19. Long tube-like mouthparts adapted for sucking—refer to No. 20
Not as above—refer to No. 22

20. Wings: when at rest held tent-like over the body.

Wings: when at rest held flat—

refer to No. 21

21. Wings: 1st pair horny, opaque at base but membranous at the apex; hind wings membranous. Head: sucking mouthparts at front of head.

HEMIPTERA
HETEROPTERA (True Bugs) ...... p. 80

22. Wings: 1st pair thickened, narrow and opaque, hind pair membranous and held folded fan-like beneath 1st pair. Legs: hind pair large and adapted for jumping. *Female:* large external ovipositor.

ORTHOPTERA
SALTATORIA (Grasshoppers,
　　　　　　Crickets) .... p. 61

Wings: 1st pair not narrow. Legs: posterior not adapted for jumping—
refer to No. 23

23. (a) Wings: 1st pair modified into short, leathery wing covers (tegmina), hind wings semi-circular and folded beneath the tegmina. Abdomen: apex terminates in forceps.

DERMAPTERA
(Earwigs) .... p. 68

(b) Wings: wing covers (tegmina) overlap. Head: invisible from above, mouthparts point backwards; antennae long, many-segmented and threadlike. Abdomen: terminates with many-segmented 'tails'.

DICTYOPTERA
(Cockroaches) ..... p. 70

Not as above—refer to No. 24

24. Wings: both pairs elongate, membranous.
Head: large and prominent eyes, antennae
small.

ODONATA
(Dragonflies) ..... p. 48

Wings: pairs differ—refer to No. 25

25. Wings: fore and hind wings similar, with
numerous cross-veins; held tent-like when
at rest. Body: soft. Head: usually with long
antennae; biting mouthparts. Abdomen:
no cerci ('tails').

NEUROPTERA
(Alder Flies,
Lace-wings) ...... p. 89

26. (a) Wings: hind pair small, triangular, held
upwards when at rest. Body: soft. Head:
antennae small and hair-like. Abdomen:
terminates in 2 or 3 long hair-like 'tails'.

EPHEMEROPTERA
(Mayflies) .... p. 45

(b) Wings: hind pair large, held flat over
back when at rest. Head: antennae long
and setaceous (bristly). Abdomen: terminates in pair of stout anal lobes.

PLECOPTERA
(Stoneflies) .... p. 59

(c) Wings: with short hairs or scales; fore
wings long, hind pair broader. Body: moth-
like. Head: antennae setaceous (bristly).
Legs: tarsi 5-segmented.

TRICHOPTERA
(Caddis Flies) .... p. 117

THE SUB-CLASS *APTERYGOTA*

The four orders of primitive wingless insects included in this sub-class are of world-wide distribution. There are some 2,300 described species, and some of these are represented in the British Isles, though they are on the whole little known because of their small size and retiring habits. (They are described here on pages 39–44.) Many more species will undoubtedly be added to the list of those already known to science. These very small insects are primitive survivals and so have little metamorphosis, indeed it is often absent; any change that does occur is gradual.

BRISTLE-TAILS Order Thysanura

Description. All small insects. Mouthparts ectognathous (exposed), adapted for biting. Antennae long, many-jointed. Compound eyes present or absent. Abdomen 11-segmented. Metamorphosis wanting or gradual. Colour brown, grey or white.

Classification. Two families comprise this order: the *Machilidae* have large compound eyes and ocelli (simple eyes). The *Lepismatidae* have small eyes and no ocelli. (9 British species).

In this widely distributed order are included the most primitive insects alive today. They are little known to amateur naturalists, and relatively few experts have studied them. Bristle-tails live under stones, in rotting wood, under wallpaper and amongst the dead leaves in woods, as well as in the soil. They are also to be found in the nests of ants, as well as (abroad) in those of termites. The best

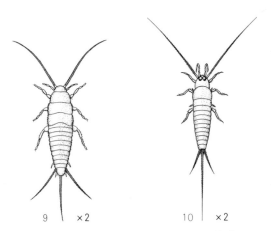

9 \ ×2   10 | ×2

Bristle-tails: **9** Silverfish, *Lepisma saccharina*. **10** *Petrobius maritimus*

known is the common Silverfish, *Lepisma saccharina*, (**9**), which finds its way into our houses from grocery stores, or in paper and books, to which it is destructive. There is also an interesting species, *Petrobius maritimus* (**10**), which is found among rocks near the edge of the sea along the British coast. The baker's 'fire brat', *Thermobia domestica*, also belongs to this order; it is remarkable for the heat it can bear. The food of bristle-tails includes sugars, starches, leaf mould and humus.

TWO-PRONGED BRISTLE-TAILS Order Diplura

Description. Resemble the previous order, the THYSANURA, but differ in the mouthparts which are entognathous (hidden, in a deep pouch); also, they have only two cerci or 'tails' which vary according to species, and there are no eyes. (12 British species).

Classification. The Diplura were formerly classed as a sub-order of the Thysanura, called Entognatha.

These tiny creatures, measuring only 3–4 mm long, have the cerci long and divided into many segments, just like their antennae, so that they may well be described as 'fore-and-aft-antennae' insects. The hidden mouthparts was the main reason for separating them from the Thysanura which have a visible, exposed mouth structure typical of other insects. When the two orders were one the Thysanura formed the first sub-order called Ectognatha.

The British species are contained in one genus, *Campodea*, among which is included the minute species *Campodea silvestrii* (**11**). The structure of the larvae of many insects resembles in form that of this very primitive insect, and this has given rise to the term *campodeiform*. Such larvae have the head,

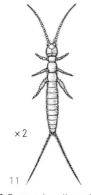

×2

×2

11 *Campodea silvestrii.* **12** larva of Great Diving Beetle,
Dytiscus marginalis

thorax and abdomen well-defined, and they possess only three pairs of legs; they are active in habit. An example is the larva of the Great Diving Beetle, *Dytiscus marginalis* (**12**). The other type of larva is termed eruciform; in this the three major divisions are not evident, and in addition to the thoracic legs there may be prolegs. Examples of this eruciform type are shown in the larvae of Lepidoptera (butterflies and moths) (**107–9**). Many eruciform larvae, however, have no legs, or, where legs are present, they may be only vestigial; examples of this type are the larvae of Diptera (two-winged flies) (**146–52**).

The Diplura live concealed but are widely distributed, occurring in the soil, among fallen leaves and under stones; when these are lifted they quickly hurry away for shelter.

Order Protura (Myrientomata)

Description. Very small species. Mouthparts sunk within the head and adapted for piercing. Antennae and compound eyes wanting. Abdomen 11-segmented. Metamorphosis slight.

Classification. The species of this order are divided into three families (20 British species).

It is not surprising that the members of this order are little known, the largest species being not 2 mm (approximately one-sixteenth of an inch) long, and this small size accounts for the lack of a popular name. They are, however, by no means rare, in fact they are widely distributed in Europe and the United States, and they are also found in India. Protura live in certain moist soils, such as peat and turf, and they have also been found under stones and beneath bark. These creatures have a habit of holding the fore legs in front of the head, and it is thought that the legs function as tactile organs, since there are no antennae. The absence of antennae is one of the reasons some naturalists maintain that the Protura form a class of their own, the Myrientomata. The figure illustrating Protura is *Acerentomon doderoi* (**13**) (much magnified).

SPRINGTAILS Order Collembola

Description. Mouthparts sunk within the head, principally adapted for biting. Antennae usually 4-jointed. Abdomen 6-segmented mostly with 3 pairs of appendages. No metamorphosis. Colour varies from white to black; there are also green, yellow, red and some banded species.

Classification. Two sub-orders, ARTHROPLEONA, having segmentation of the abdomen well defined, and SYMPHYPLEONA, having vestigial or no segmentation of abdomen. (304 British species).

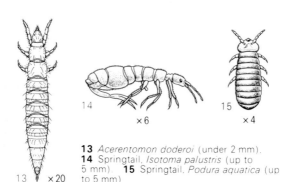

13 *Acerentomon doderoi* (under 2 mm).
14 Springtail, *Isotoma palustris* (up to 5 mm). **15** Springtail, *Podura aquatica* (up to 5 mm)

43

Springtails are named after their method of leaping to a distance of several inches when disturbed. They congregate in vast numbers. A well-known entomologist, John Ford, found that a hectare of meadow-land, to a depth of 23 cm (9 inches), contained 575,000,000 of these insects. They are also to be found beneath the bark of trees, in decaying vegetable matter, and so on, especially if conditions are moist. Springtails render invaluable help in sewage farms, where they feed on decaying matter. *Anurida maritima* lives along the coast and is submerged at high tide. It is one of the few marine insects; it has not the modified springing legs characteristic of other Collembola (**14, 15**).

The springtail *Podura aquatica*, described by Linnaeus as long ago as 1758, was one of the favourite 'objects of the microscope' prepared for sale during the heyday of amateur microscopy in the last century. Members of the species are found on stagnant pools, where they may be seen jerking about on the surface of the water.

Most species are small, rarely exceeding a length of 5 mm ($\frac{3}{16}$ in).

THE SUB-CLASS *PTERYGOTA*

The remaining insect orders described in this book all form part of the second sub-class, the *PTERYGOTA*, or Winged Insects. This group is by far the largest into which the Insecta are divided. Its members differ essentially from the Apterygota (p. 39) in that they are winged insects, though included with them are secondary wingless forms, such as those of the important order Siphonaptera (fleas). The wings of insects are of two types: (i) those that cannot be folded; when at rest they are held extended erect above the body and they cannot be flexed over the abdomen. This is the primitive type; the insects exhibiting this peculiarity are called Palaeoptera, represented today by the dragonflies and mayflies. (ii) The second type of wing—belonging to the Neoptera—can be folded over the abdomen; there are many examples. It constitutes the principal type today. The ability to flex the wings has been lost again among Lepidoptera, and indeed some of them have even become wingless.

The power of flight has given these insects—the first flying animals—a great advantage: it has enabled them to move quickly from one feeding area to another and to escape more easily from their enemies. In several species, loss of wings has followed highly evolved specialization which has often brought about actual degeneration. In this sub-class there are no abdominal appendages, other than genitalia and cerci ('tails').

The *PTERYGOTA* develop their wings either externally (*EXOPTERYGOTA*: pages 45–88), or internally (*ENDOPTERYGOTA*: pages 88–171). In the latter the wings become visible only in the adult (imago) stage.

Division (a) *EXOPTERYGOTA*

MAYFLIES Order Ephemeroptera

Description. Body soft. Mouthparts vestigial. Antennae short and bristly. Abdomen long terminating in three long cerci, 'tails'. Four membranous wings,

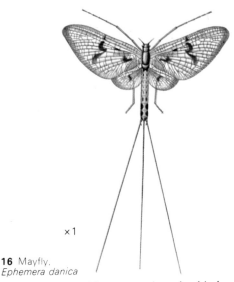

×1

16 Mayfly,
Ephemera danica

transparent, with many veins, the hind pair much reduced in size. Wings held vertically upwards when at rest. Metamorphosis incomplete but unique in that the imagines (adults) have a winged sub-imago stage. Nymphs aquatic.

Classification. The order comprises thirteen families, eight of which are British. They are grouped into three superfamilies. (47 British species).

Mayflies are common round the margins of inland waters. They may often be seen in large swarms at the end of May and the beginning of June. They are particularly well known to anglers, who refer to them as 'duns', 'spinners' and 'drakes'. These are used as bait, and artificial copies of them are made to serve the same purpose. All anglers'

46

'flies' are not mayflies, for they also include stone-flies and caddis flies, though the majority of species do belong to the order Ephemeroptera.

The brief life of a mayfly is proverbial. It may last but a few hours, though this is of course true only of the adult winged form. The nymph, which is entirely aquatic, may have lived as long as three years before completing its larval stage of development. Nymphs of *Ephemera* (**17**), *Ecdyonurus* (**18**) and *Cloeon* (**19**) are shown.

The nymphs vary much in form, depending on whether they live in still or running water, and this has a direct bearing on the genera to be found there. The nymphs feed mainly on minute vegetable matter, such as algae and diatoms, in addition to fragments of other plant tissues. Some species prefer to live where there are sandy beds, whilst others are to be found in silt or moss, in the decaying vegetation of ditches, in fact, almost

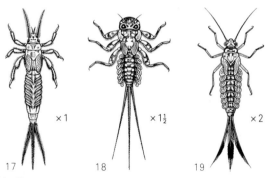

×1 ×1½ ×2

17 18 19

Mayfly nymphs: **17** *Ephemera*, **18** *Ecdyonurus*,. **19** *Cloeon* everywhere. They breathe by means of tracheal gills, which vary much in form and are attached externally to the abdominal segments.

The fully developed nymph floats to the surface of the water in late spring or early summer, or it climbs out on to a stone or up a plant. Here the nymphal case splits open, and from it emerges a winged insect, but unlike the similar process in other insects, this is not yet the final stage of its life-history. It has only attained the stage known as the sub-imago, unique in insect metamorphosis. The sub-imago is dull-coloured; it is the 'dun' of the angler. It flies away to rest among vegetation, and later the final moult takes place, disclosing the fully-coloured mayfly or 'spinner' (**16**).

Swarms of males of many species engage in a dancing flight, which is rhythmic up-and-down movement, and takes place at certain times of the day. On the approach of a female some of the males go towards her; pairing takes place in 'nuptial flight'. Many mayflies are nocturnal in habit.

The eggs are dropped into the water, or the abdomen is dipped below the surface, and in some species the insect actually penetrates into the water to lay her eggs. Mayfly eggs are remarkable for the diversity of their structure.

DRAGONFLIES AND DAMSELFLIES
Order Odonata

Description. Large or moderate sized predaceous insects. Body long, often slender. Head large with very large and prominent eyes. Antennae thin and very short. Four wings approximately same size and membranous with many veins. Metamorphosis incomplete. Nymphs aquatic.

Classification. Two distinct sub-orders: The ZYGOP-TERA, damselflies, close their wings (with very few exceptions) vertically above the abdomen when at rest. Fore and hind wings resemble each other closely, their bases being narrow. Nymphs have three tail-like projections which are gills, absent in nymphs of Anisoptera. The *ANISOPTERA*, dragonflies, hold the wings open when at rest, the fore wings differing in shape from the hind pair, which are broader near the base. The space between the eyes is always smaller than their own diameter. (42 British species).

The brilliantly coloured, sun-loving dragonfly is noted for the speed of its flight—in one species this is said to attain sixty miles an hour! It is a fearsome hunter of other insects which are caught and devoured in flight. The damselfly is a much more delicate insect, and may even be quite a weak flier. It is certainly not the countryman's 'Horse Stinger' or 'Devil's Darning Needle', popular names which must assuredly have been given by non-naturalists to the much more powerful species of dragonflies (sub-order Anisoptera), though no member of the order Odonata has a sting. Of the dragonflies, *Libellula quadrimaculata* (25) is an example of a migratory species, large numbers of them having been recorded as travelling many miles out to sea, though on the whole dragonflies do not wander far from their breeding-place; many may, however, frequently be found farther from stretches of water than the majority of insects having aquatic larvae. Damselflies are normally found only near water.

The nymphs of this order are well known to collectors of pond life. Specimens are popular though often very destructive inmates of an amateur's aquarium, and their habits at this stage of their life-history are therefore better known than are those of the adult insect. Nymphs of the two sub-orders are easily distinguishable from each other, for the dragonfly nymph has a more robust structure (**27–38**) than that of the damselfly (**39–44**) which is slender, and has in addition three long 'tails' which are breathing gills. Both nymphs are carnivorous, possessing a 'mask' (**20–21**) consisting of impaling mandibles or hooks on an extensible limb, which is used for bringing the food to the mouth and for holding it there. The mask is shown at rest, **20,** and extended, **21**; it is shot out with lightning speed when prey of suitable size approaches within reach, and the nymph may also dart forward to seize its victim, but at other times the creature is sluggish. It is difficult to detect a nymph because it possesses most effective protective coloration, and this may even change according to environment.

Some of the more common nymphs found when collecting from ponds are shown. Although metamorphosis is incomplete in this order, it will be seen from these illustrations that the fully grown

Mask of Dragonfly nymph: **20** at rest. **21** extended

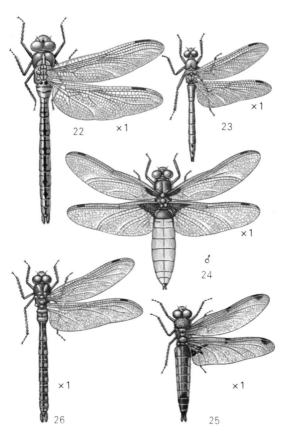

Dragonflies. **22** *Anax imperator.* **23** *Sympetrum strio-latum.* **24** *Libellula depressa* male. **25** *L. quadrimaculata.* **26** *Aeschna junaea*

nymphs do not bear a close resemblance to the adult insects (**22–26, 45–49**) as is the case, for example, in grasshoppers and bugs. This is particularly evident in the dragonflies, whose robust nymphal body does not announce the slenderness of that of the adult, nor does it indicate—as in the case of most insects—any of the wonderful coloration to come.

The nymph leaves the water after a larval period of about a year in the case of the damselflies (Zygoptera) and two years in that of the dragonflies (Anisoptera). It then climbs up a reed or other projection above the surface. Here the final transformation takes place, the nymphal skin splits and the imago wriggles out. The wings then expand and the abdomen becomes elongate and slender; the coloration takes a certain time to develop, and this waiting or 'teneral' period may last for several days.

The mating of the adults is most curious. It takes place in flight, on the ground, or among vegetation, depending on the genus. The male has special anal claspers which are used for gripping the female in the back of the head or neck. The extraordinary pairing attitude adopted in this order of Odonata is necessary because the orifices of the male and female genitalia are situated at widely separated parts of the body.

The eggs are laid in water, sometimes inside plant stems. The females of some species penetrate below the surface for egg-laying, and are helped in doing this by the male, who remains above the surface whilst keeping a firm grasp on the female.

As the nymphal instar (stage) is more often studied than the adult instar (because it is possible to confine nymphs most conveniently in an aquarium where they may be kept under close observation), we give below a few details of some of the commoner nymphs collected from ponds and streams.

Nymphs of Dragonflies (Sub-Order Anisoptera)

(The measurements given of nymphs indicate the length of the body, including the tail-like gills, but excluding the antennae. Where equivalent measurements are given in inches, these are approximate, to the nearest sixteenth of an inch).

Cordulegaster boltonii (**27**). Attains 41 mm ($1\frac{5}{8}$ in). Under the debris of rapid-moving water, sometimes in mud. Only common locally, mostly in the West, South of Scotland, and in the southern counties. Imago seen from the end of June to the beginning of September. The dragonfly has circles of black and yellow bands, and is one of our largest species.

The Hairy Dragonfly   *Brachytron pratense* (**28**). Attains 40 mm ($1\frac{9}{16}$ in). Mainly in England and Wales, in ponds, etc., on sticks and debris to which it holds closely. Imago is on the wing from May to the middle of July. Female dark brown.

The Emperor Dragonfly   *Anax imperator* (**29**). Attains 54 mm ($2\frac{1}{8}$ in). Most waters especially among reeds, but common only in the Southeast. Absent from Scotland, doubtful in Ireland. Imago (the Emperor Dragonfly) (**22**) is seen especially in June and July. This is one of our three largest species, and in appearance resembles those of the genus *Aeshna* (*see* following).

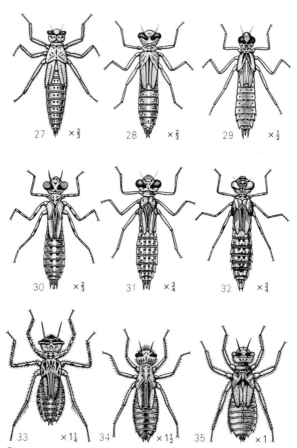

Dragonfly nymphs: **27** *Cordulegaster boltonii.*
28 *Brachytron pratense.* **29** *Anax imperator.* **30** *Aeshna cyanea.* **31** *A. juncea.* **32** *A. grandis.* **33** *Cordulia aenea.*
34 *Orthetrum coerulescens.* **35** *Libellula quadrimaculata*

The Southern Hawker   *Aeshna cyanea* (**30**).
Attains 48 mm ($1\frac{7}{8}$ in). Very common in the
southern counties on weeds in still waters. Absent
from Scotland and Ireland. Imago is seen from
summer to autumn, especially July and August.

The Common Hawker   *Aeshna juncea* (**31**).
Attains 43 mm ($1\frac{11}{16}$ in). Common on weeds in
ponds, also peat pools in mountains. The adult
(**26** male) attacks other insects, including
dragon- and damselflies. Common from the end
of July and during August. Its colour varies with
age and sex.

The Brown Hawker   *Aeshna grandis* (**32**). Attains 43 mm ($1\frac{11}{16}$ in). Common only in midland
and southern counties, on pond weeds. Imago
seen towards end July/August. The dragonfly is
entirely brown in colour. It flies until dark.

The Downy Emerald   *Cordulia aenea* (**33**). Attains 22 mm ($\frac{7}{8}$ in). Conceals itself among debris
in slow-moving waters where there are reeds and
rushes. Imago emerges in June. It is bronze-green
in colour, eyes brilliant emerald-green.

The Keeled Skimmer   *Orthetrum coerulescens*
(**34**). Attains 19 mm ($\frac{3}{4}$ in). Especially in pools on
moors in southern counties, but recorded in
Inverness, fairly common in Ireland. The imago
is blue and emerges chiefly in July and August.

The Four-spotted Libellula   *Libellula quadrimaculata* (**35**). Attains 26 mm (1 in). Very common locally in pool debris. Imago (**25**) is on the
wing in spring and early summer, particularly in

55

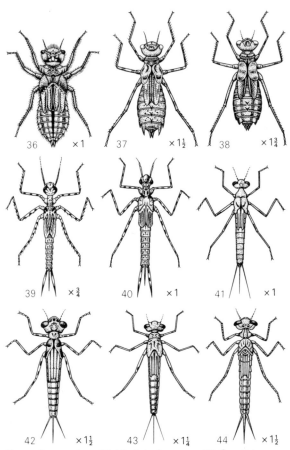

Dragonfly nymphs: **36** *Libellula depressa*, **37** *Sympetrum striolatum*, **38** *S. danae*; Damselfly nymphs: **39** *Calopteryx virgo*, **40** *C. splendens*, **41** *Lestes sponsa*, **42** *Pyrrhosoma nymphula*, **43** *Ischnura elegans*, **44** *Enallagma cyathigerum*

56

June and July. Its numbers are increased by immigrants. Variable in size and colouring.

The Broad-bodied Libellula   *Libellula depressa* (**36**). Attains 25 mm (1 in). Very common in the south, absent from north-west England, Scotland and Ireland. Lives in the debris of ditches, ponds and lakes. Imago (**24** male) is seen especially in June and July. Colour variable.

The Common Darter   *Sympetrum striolatum* (**37**). Attains 18 mm ($\frac{3}{4}$ in). Common in mud and weeds of ponds. Imago (**23**) is on the wing in late summer and autumn. It is chiefly red and yellow-brown, or the red may be absent.

The Black Darter   *Sympetrum danae* (**38**). Attains 15 mm ($\frac{9}{16}$ in). Common in lakes and boggy ponds having reeds and rushes, particularly in Scotland. The species is more common where there are moors and marshes.

Nymphs of Damselflies (Sub-Order Zygoptera)

The Beautiful Demoiselle   *Calopteryx virgo* (**39**). Attains 32 mm ($1\frac{1}{4}$ in). Widely distributed and very common in the South. Prefers running water, but also found in ponds. Imago on the wing in spring and summer, most common in June and July. The male is the most beautiful of the damselflies, of varied colour. The female is quite different, being emerald green.

The Banded Demoiselle   *Calopteryx splendens* (**40**). Attains 32 mm ($1\frac{1}{4}$ in). Common from the Mid-

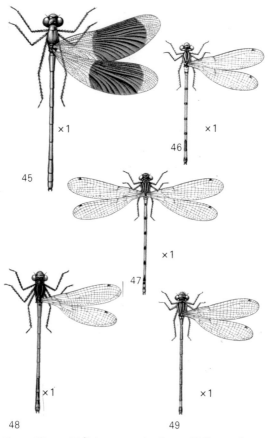

×1

×1

46

45

×1

47

×1

48

×1

49

Damselflies: **45** *Calopteryx splendens*, **46** *Coenagrion puella*,
47 *Enallagma cyathigerum*, **48** *Pyrrhosoma nymphula*,
49 *Ischnura elegans*

58

lands to the South, and in most of Wales and Ireland. Absent from Scotland. Imago (the Banded Agrion) most common in June and July. As in the case of *A. virgo*, the male (**45**) differs much in colour from the female.

The Emerald Damselfly   *Lestes sponsa* (**41**). Attains 26 mm (1 in). Among vegetation of ponds and ditches, also in brackish water. It is common, although rare in the Home Counties and in the Midlands. Imago commonest in August.

The Large Red Damselfly   *Pyrrhosoma nymphula* (**42**). Attains 19 mm ($\frac{3}{4}$ in). Found in quiet waters, also in brackish water. Very common. Imago (**48**, female) is on the wing from May to July.

The Blue-Tailed Damselfly   *Ischnura elegans* (**43**). Attains 20 mm ($\frac{3}{4}$ in). On vegetation in slow-moving waters. Exceedingly common. Imago (the common Ischnura) is on the wing from May to August; it is slender, and dark greenish-black.

The Common Blue Damselfly   *Enallagma cyathigerum* (**44**). Attains 20 mm ($\frac{3}{4}$ in). Very common on water-weeds. Bright green, occasionally brown. Imago (**47**) seen in June, July and August.

STONEFLIES Order Plecoptera

Description. Moderate sized or large insects. Body soft. Long antennae. Weak biting mouth parts. Four membranous wings with numerous veins; wings held flat over body when at rest. Abdomen usually with long jointed cerci, 'tails'. Metamorphosis incomplete, pupal stage absent. Nymphs aquatic. Colour brown.

Classification. A small order, three of the seven families being represented in the British Isles (34 British species).

Stoneflies are on the whole little known to the majority of people. This is due to the rather restricted habitat of these insects. Their aquatic larvae require clean, well-oxygenated water. They are found beneath the stones of mountain streams, and near waterfalls. The nymphs climb out of the water when full-grown, and the final transformation into the imago then takes place, very much in the manner of dragonflies.

The adults are fairly large. What makes them also particularly noticeable to the non-naturalist is that their flight attracts attention to itself by its slowness; the insects are weak fliers, and when touched they fall to the ground. Stoneflies never wander far from water, and will be found at rest on anything suitable in the neighbourhood, including stones, fences, bridges and so on. The adults are short-lived, like mayflies, and apparently they do not feed,

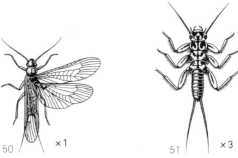

50 | ×1   51 | ×3

50 Stonefly, *Diura bicaudata*, **51** its nymph

the mouth parts being almost useless. The female usually lays her eggs in one mass, and in some species there may be as many as 2,000 eggs. These become detached from each other in the water, and eventually adhere to stones and plants by means of a long thread with which each egg is provided.

Stoneflies may be readily distinguished from members of the order Neuroptera (page 89) by the cerci or 'tails' present in the adults. Also the wings are held flat over the body (**50**) whilst Neuroptera hold them roof-wise.

GRASSHOPPERS AND CRICKETS Order Orthoptera

Description. Mouthparts adapted for biting or chewing. Usually four wings, the fore pair being modified into hardened wing-cases (tegmina) which protect the hind pair when at rest. Hind wings membranous and transparent. Hind legs usually enlarged and of the jumping kind. Abdomen with short and usually unsegmented cerci or 'tails', but not always evident. Ovipositor generally present and prominent. Metamorphosis slight or absent. Colour: brown, greens.

Classification. There are two sub-orders, the ENSIFERA and the CAELIFERA, respectively the long-horned and the short-horned orthopterans. (30 British species).

The order used to divide into two sub-orders, the Cursoria, the Runners, and the Saltatoria, or Jumpers; these latter remain in the present order. The Cursoria or cockroaches are now included in a new order called Dictyoptera described on p. 70.

The formerly-called Saltatoria are represented by our common summer-loving grasshoppers and tiresome house crickets. They differ essentially

61

from cockroaches in having the third pair of legs powerfully developed for jumping and leaping, these limbs being most important for allowing the nymphs, which cannot yet fly, to escape from danger by leaping. Furthermore, many species remain wingless on reaching the adult stage. Grasshoppers emerge in May from eggs laid the previous year in capsules of dried mucus; they are fully grown by midsummer and live until September.

There are two kinds of grasshopper in the British Isles, the short-horned and the long-horned, named after the length of the antennae. The short-horned, of which we have fourteen native species, belong to the family Acrididae. They are vegetarians, and include some of our commonest species. They are also the noisiest of our grasshoppers. The volume of their 'song' or stridulation (see page 19) is in direct proportion to the heat and amount of sunshine, and they are indeed our summer songsters, the equivalent of the Mediterranean cicadas. These Acridids occur in all parts of the world and some of them are among the greatest of all insect pests, for the foreign locusts are of their number. One of the commonest species is *Omocestus viridulus* which will be found especially on the grassy slopes of downs. It is dull olive-green in colour.

Our long-horned species belong to the family Tettigoniidae, and are also popularly known as bush crickets. They differ in several respects from the short-horned. Besides the obvious difference in length of the antennae, they have their ears situated in the fore legs. The short-horned have their ears or (membranous) tympana situated on the first abdominal segment. The method of stridulation is also quite different. The long-horned rub parts of the wings together, as we have already seen, whereas the short-horned use their legs on the fore-wings for the purpose. The long-horned are not specialized in diet and are very frequently carnivorous,

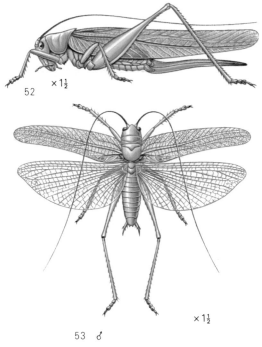

52 × 1½

53 ♂ × 1½

Great Green Grasshopper. *Tettigonia viridissima:* **52** female. **53** male attacking other insects as well as their own kind. They hunt mainly at night and bite the victim just behind the neck. The largest of our grasshoppers belongs to this family; it is the Great Green Grasshopper, *Tettigonia viridissima* (**52–3**), in which the method of pairing is among the most curious of the insect world and has been described at length by the incomparable French naturalist Fabre.

The crickets (family Gryllidae), although closely related to the long-horned grasshoppers, may be distinguished from them and the other foregoing species by their long cerci or tails, and by the hardened fore wings, which lie flat over the abdomen, and downwards along the sides. Furthermore, the right fore wing lies over the left, which is contrary to what usually obtains in this order. The stridulating apparatus is also relatively larger than in the long-horned grasshoppers. The best known of the crickets is common: the House Cricket, *Acheta domestica* (**54**) also known as the cricket on the hearth. It is found fairly frequently in or near warm places. There is also the lesser known *Gryllus campestris* (**55**) a field species which has a

54 House
Cricket.
*Acheta
domestica*.
55 Field
Cricket.
*Gryllus
campestris*

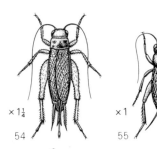

× 1¼

× 1

54

55

×1

56 Mole Cricket, *Gryllotalpa gryllotalpa*

burrow home, and which is the insect made famous by Fabre's description of its habits. This species, popularly known as the Field Cricket, is black in colour with a yellow band across the base of the elytra; the head is big and broad. It will be found sitting at the mouth of its lair chirping merrily away on hot days from the middle of May to the middle of July. It is now very local in distribution.

The most unusual cricket in appearance is the Mole Cricket, *Gryllotalpa gryllotalpa* (**56**) (family Gryllotalpidae). Subterranean in habit, it may have become extinct in Britain, but is a most interesting species, showing much morphological modification. The strong fore legs have become adapted for burrowing and, with the front part of the body, which is armoured, are therefore in keeping with its habits. The mole cricket lays her eggs in a mass, placing them in a cavity and remaining in attendance. However, when the eggs hatch, the parent seems to destroy some of the progeny. Gilbert White, in his *Natural History of Selborne*, gives a most interesting account of finding the 'nest' or egg-mass of this insect.

STICK INSECTS, LEAF INSECTS Order Phasmida

Description. Large insects with or without wings. Of the three thoracic segments the first (prothorax) is short, the other two (mesothorax and metathorax) are

65

usually long, a marked character. Legs: similar to each other. Cerci short. In British species the body is long, slender, and approximately the same width throughout.

Classification. In the British Isles there are only introduced species. The order comprises three families. (Three British species).

Two of the three introduced species come from New Zealand; the other is from the oriental region; and as they have become truly established here they are now on the British list. Stick-insects are the only members of the Phasmida that occur here. The leaf-insects do not. These belong to the family Phylliidae, the more spectacular members of the

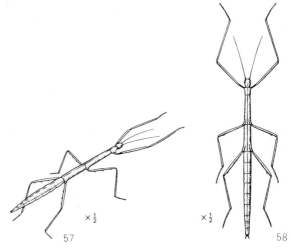

Stick Insects: **57** *Carausius morosus,* **58** *Clitarchus hookeri*

order; they are well known because of their marvellous resemblance to leaves. However, the stick-insects themselves may also be relied upon to excite general interest as they are equally camouflaged in appearance. They look like twigs. They are vegetarian and nocturnal in habits and though motionless on bushes during daytime they may at times be seen swaying from side to side. Why they do this is not known. *Carausius morosus* (**57**) is much used for teaching and research and is thus popularly known as the Laboratory Stick-insect; it is also kept as a pet. In captivity it is fed on privet, but will also eat other evergreens such as holly and ivy. It has established itself in South Devon and Surrey. Its coloration is green or brown, sometimes almost black. It has no dorsal black line which distinguishes it from the Smooth Stick-insect, *Clitarchus hookeri* (**58**), which immigrated to these shores from New Zealand. This species has established itself in gardens in Tresco, Scilly Isles, as has also the New Zealand Spiny Stick-insect, *Acanthoxyla prasina*, which has spines on most parts of the body.

A peculiarity of these insects is that the pairing of the sexes is unnecessary for reproduction. Indeed in the case of the most studied species, *Carausius morosus*, males are practically unknown; less than twenty have so far been recorded. The successful reproduction of offspring from unfertilized eggs is termed parthenogenesis. The eggs, which are very hard, are dropped singly and haphazardly; they are large, having an operculum (cap) which is pushed open by the emerging young insect. The eggs take a long time to hatch, up to a year or more.

Description. Long body, Biting mouthparts. Antennae long, many jointed. Fore wings modified into short wing-cases, hind wings folded and for flying. Many wingless forms. Cerci unjointed, forming the familiar pincers or forceps. Metamorphosis slight or absent. Colour, browns and black.

Classification. Three sub-orders, only one, the *FORFICULINA*, earwigs, being represented in the British Isles. The others, the *ARIXENIINA* and *HEMIMERINA*, are tropical and all species are blind external parasites of bats and rats. (9 British species).

Our commonest earwig, *Forficula auricularia* (male—**60**, female—**61**, male shown with a wing extended—**59**) is so decidedly distinctive in appearance that we recognize it at the first glance. It is not often that a creature of mostly nocturnal habit is so well known, even to non-naturalists. In daylight it conceals itself, often among the petals of flowers, particularly when these are large and luxuriant, as in the case of dahlias, and thus it is that earwigs are frequently disturbed and seen. The name 'earwig' too helps us to bear it well in mind, although to the scientist it is puzzling. It is thought to have its origin in the fact that these insects could wander into the ear of a person at rest, the ear cavity being a suitable place for concealment. Should this occur, it certainly results in consternation and physical irritation, but that they are actually ear-piercers, as they are called in French, is considered to be mere calumniation of a highly interesting insect.

Earwigs have no constriction between the thorax and the abdomen, but the most marked features are the forceps or pincers which terminate the abdomen. There is much variation in the shape of the pincers, and they also differ between the sexes, those of the female being less curved. There are several theories regarding the use of these instruments. They are often thought to be organs of offence and defence, for they may sometimes be seen protruding jaw-like in places where the insect is hiding, and an earwig may certainly be seen raising the pincers when alarmed. It has also been said that the pincers are used for folding and unfolding the wings. The wings are complicated, and seem to be infrequently used, and are remarkable for the manner in which they are literally folded and tucked away under the wing-cases.

The Common Earwig is found throughout the British Isles and remarkable observations have been made about it. Hibernation occurs in the adult stage and usually a male and a female are found together. They will be found in small galleries, under stones and other sheltered places. Here pairing occurs frequently. Eggs are laid between January and March; the male then leaves the nest, perhaps driven away. The earwig lays comparatively few eggs, about two dozen. They are smooth and pale coloured, and they are brooded over by the female very much as in the case of the hen. The eggs are laid in mid-winter, under a stone or other suitable cover, but always in a damp situation. Here the eggs would soon be attacked by mildew were this not prevented by the mother, who licks each egg clean once every day.

The life-history of the earwig was studied as long ago as the middle of the eighteenth century by

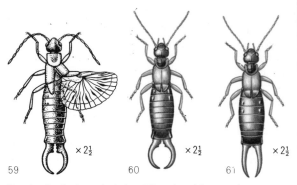

Earwig, *Forficula auricularia*: **59** male, with one wing extended, **60** male, **61** female

Baron de Geer. He scattered the eggs, and found that the female collected them together again, carrying them in her mouth. On hatching, the young remain with their mother and place themselves "under her belly, like little chicks under a hen", which was what had originally attracted this naturalist to earwigs more closely.

COCKROACHES Order Dictyoptera

Description. Cockroaches when seen from above have the head hidden or nearly so by a large hood-like plate, the pronotum. Long threadlike antennae with many joints. Legs: resemble each other; tarsi 5-segmented. Wings: in British species fully developed and membranous, or merely vestigial. Short, jointed cerci.

Classification. There are two sub-orders, the *BLATTARIA* (or Blattodea), the cockroaches, comprising one large family, *Blattidae*, and the non-British *MANTODEA*, the praying mantids. The latter differ in many ways from the above description of the cockroaches. (8 British species).

The unpleasant cockroaches were formerly included in the Orthoptera in a division called Cursoria, the Runners. Most of these insects are actually natives of frost-free habitats which have become established here, but only where continuous warmth is assured, such as in bakeries, hotel kitchens and at zoological gardens in animal cages, which are kept at warm temperatures. They are most readily seen behind the glass where snakes are kept, and seem actually to be 'tame' there and, contrary to their usual habits, forget that they are supposed to be nocturnal. Here they may certainly be studied at leisure. The female lays her eggs in an egg-case (*ootheca*) which may sometimes be seen protruding from the abdomen. An example of such a female is shown in the illustration of our commonest species, *Blatta orientalis* (**62**). Observing the long and many-jointed antennae of a living cockroach, and the way they move about nervously and deliberately, we can deduce the very great importance of these organs to the insect.

Cockroaches eat all kinds of foods, especially those that are sweet and starchy. They are destructive pests, and they foul stored foodstuffs, being particularly obnoxious because of their stink-glands. The unpleasant smell of cockroaches persists wherever they have been.

BOOKLICE Order Psocoptera

Description. Very small insects. Biting mouthparts. Winged or wingless. Long antennae, having nine or more joints. Membranous wings. Segments of thorax very distinct. Metamorphosis gradual or absent.

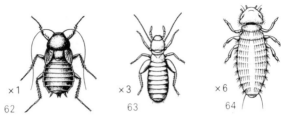

62 Cockroach, *Blatta orientalis*. **63** Booklouse, *Liposcelis granicola* (up to 6 mm). **64** Chicken Louse, *Menopon gallinae* (under 6 mm)

Classification. The British species of Psocoptera belong to the largest super-family *EUPSOCIDA*. (70 British species).

Though cerci or 'tails' may be present in other super-families, they are absent in the species found in the British Isles; the antennae have many segments, from twenty to as many as fifty. At times the species may be very numerous indeed, especially in undisturbed places, such as in empty houses. Many are gregarious in habit.

Among these tiny insects are the very minute whitish creatures (*Liposcelis divinatorius*) found in old books and papers. They are the booklice, whose food consists of book-paste as well as decaying vegetable and animal matter. Not all our native species have the same feeding habits; some live on dry farm refuse and a number of stored cereals, others live out of doors on tree-trunks, fences, beneath bark, on moss, lichen and other vegetation. Psocoptera are important distributors of spores of fungi. Some forms are winged, and are easily confused with aphids. A wingless example of the order is *Liposcelis granicola* (**63**).

72

Description. Very small flattened insects. Wingless. Antennae short, 3- to 5-jointed. Mouthparts adapted for biting. Of the 3 thoracic segments the first only is distinctly free. Legs short and adapted for clinging to host. No metamorphosis. Parasites of mammals and birds. Colour whitish-yellow or darker.

Classification. Formerly divided into two sub-orders, Mallophaga, biting lice, and Siphunculata, sucking lice. The status of these two divisions has been raised to that of separate orders, the main difference between them being concerned with the method of feeding, whether the species bites or sucks—the anatomical features of the mouthparts constituting great differences where classification is concerned. There are 514 British species of Mallophaga.

Species of the order Mallophaga, the biting lice, are found mostly on birds, and are well known to bird fanciers. A few species are found on mammals. Biting lice feed on the products of the skin. In birds they are particularly destructive to the feathers, and in severe cases this may result in bald patches. The very common Chicken Louse, *Menopon gallinae* (**64**) is a pest of chickens. Ducks are infested with *Anatoecus dentatus* but there are also several other lice parasites. Cats may have among their fur *Felicola subrostratus* and dogs *Trichodectes canis*.

SUCKING LICE Order Siphunculata (Anoplura)

Description. Small flattened insects. Wingless. Mouthparts adapted into styles for piercing and sucking. Antennae 3- to 5-segmented. Thoracic segments fused. Parasites of mammals.

Classification. This order of sucking lice used to be a sub-order classed with another, the biting lice, forming one order called Anoplura. (24 British species.)

Members of this order feed on the blood of mammals, each species of which has its particular kind of louse—though man shares *Pediculus* with the chimpanzee. Of the many species, some 225 in all, only two infest man; the others are obligatory parasites of other mammals including elephants and seals. Their only food is blood and they cannot survive away from their host. The Human Louse, *Pediculus humanus* (**65**) has two races, according to whether it lives on the head (sub-species or race *capitis*) or on the body (race *corporis*). The species is of great medical importance as a vector (disease carrier-transmitter) of more diseases than any other insect, including such scourges as typhus, trench fever and so on. One other species also lives on man, the Crab Louse, *Phthirus pubis*, particularly restricted to unclean people. *Pediculus* infection may originate temporarily from unclean people conveying it to others in crowded conditions in which customary cleanliness cannot be practised, as among front-line troops and prisoners.

Lice cannot live away from their host, and their highly specialized habits are reflected in their structure, such as the absence of wings and the

65 Human Louse. *Pediculus humanus (under 6 mm).*
66 claw. **67** egg

74

powerful clinging-claws (**66**). Lice glue their eggs ('nits') (**67**) to the host's hairs or to clothing, and they hatch in about eight days.

PLANT AND WATER BUGS Order Hemiptera

Description. Usually with four wings, the fore pair mostly modified to a horny consistency; the hind pair membranous and transparent. Mouthparts adapted for piercing and sucking. Metamorphosis gradual, rarely complete. Colour, great variety.

Classification. Two sub-orders, the HOMOPTERA having metamorphosis incomplete, or complete in males and incomplete in females, they have the fore wings transparent and usually slope roof-like over the sides of the body; and, the HETEROPTERA, having the fore wings horny and the hind wings transparent, the wings usually held flat and overlapping each other over the abdomen.

The HOMOPTERA are further divided into three series: (i) the COLEORRHYNCHA, (ii) the AUCHENORRHYNCHA, and (iii) the STERNORRHYNCHA. Those in the first series are found only in some parts of the southern hemisphere.

There is also a further division of the HETEROPTERA which it is useful to note. They may, for convenience, be divided into two series of species: (i) the *Gymnocerata*, the land bugs (pages 76–84), having the antennae conspicuous, and (ii) the *Cryptocerata*, the water bugs (pages 84–87), antennae concealed. There are over 1,600 British species of Hemiptera.

A marked characteristic of this order is that all species, animal and vegetable feeders alike, live by piercing and sucking at all stages of their lives. They have for this a specially developed beak (*rostrum*), which is held below against the body when not in use. The proboscis or beak consists of a sheath containing four piercers needed for making an opening into which the rostrum proper is pushed for sucking out the plant-juices, or blood in the case of a small number of carnivorous species. Bugs are also called 'Rhynchota' (*rhynchos*, proboscis), after the specialized mouth structure.

Sub-Order Homoptera
(Order Hemiptera)

Description. The important anatomical feature of this sub-order is that its members have four transparent wings (*see* page 75).

Classification. These insects are diverse in structure, and include the families *Cicadidae*—cicadas; *Cercopidae*—froghoppers or cuckoo-spit insects; *Membracidae*—treehoppers; *Cicadellidae*—leafhoppers; all are in the second series AUCHENORRHYNCHA. The third series of this sub-order are the STERNORRHYNCHA, including the many species of the gardener's plant pests, such as the *Psyllidae*—jumping plant-lice; *Aleyrodidae*—white-flies; *Aphididae*—green-fly; *Coccidae*—scale-insects, mealy-bugs.

We have all heard of the cicadas of the South of France, and of Fabre's complaints about the noise of the males. Joubert has summed up our thoughts about them: 'Sunshine and summer heat, without the accompaniment of the cicada's song, or the quivering of the air, is like a dance without music.' Nevertheless we have in the British Isles one species that does not appear to mind our climate. It is *Cicadetta montana*, but it is found only in Hampshire. This insect should be considered as a protected species. It is little known and is scarce in its English habitat, the New Forest. It emerges in late May and appears in open woodland fringes facing south. It feeds on the foliage of trees and on bracken—a common fern which is not normally relished by animals. Many eggs are laid, almost 300 have been counted by one entomologist.

Cuckoo-spit found on plants is a protective froth made by the nymphs of the broad-headed family, Cercopidae, the commonest being *Philaenus spumarius*. *Cercopis vulnerata* (**68**) is a uniquely coloured native froghopper, found in some districts on alder and sallow. Leafhoppers (family Jassidae) are extremely common and when disturbed will leap several feet, or fly away.

The most numerous individuals on plants and trees are plant-lice, green-fly, white-fly, aphids, scale-insects and mealy-bugs. These are the insects whose progeny would soon turn the world into an uninhabitable waste were it not for the havoc wrought on them by the weather, birds, etc., but most of all by other insects, both parasites and predators. They have the curious feature of discharging continuously a sugary waste known as honey-dew. This is highly attractive to ants, which procure it by making regular journeys to plants and up trees infested with these redoubtable pests; the honey-dew is also attractive to many night-flying moths.

Plant-lice and aphids have winged and wingless forms, and they live mainly on new shoots. They are remarkable for their different methods of development, for within one species they will be found to lay eggs and also to be viviparous, whilst the non-fertilization of females by males also obtains, and indeed males are often very rare in certain generations. Structure, food-plants and habits may also change from one generation to another, constituting a regular but complex series of events. One species, for example, after over-wintering as eggs laid in the autumn by sexual females, will produce wingless females which hatch from the eggs in spring, and are viviparous and parthenogenetic (i.e., no fertilization by the male necessary for fertility). From their eggs come similar females, but some are now winged, and these may fly away to infest other plants. This succession goes on during the whole season until the end of the summer or into the autumn, when sexual males and females occur, these females being once again fertilized egg-layers, so that the cycle is now complete. There are also migratory species who must change food-plants according to seasonal availability. A foreign species, *Phylloxera quercus*, has twenty-one forms!

The following are a few of the many garden and nursery pests contained in the three families of Sternorrhyncha mentioned on page 76.

The common pest of greenhouses is the Greenhouse White-fly, *Trialeurodes vaporariorum*, of the family Aleyrodidae; it is also known as the Ghost Fly. The species attacks anything growing under glass, and particularly tomatoes. The insect is a foreign immigrant which is unable to live the whole year round out-of-doors.

An all-too-common representative of the family Psyllidae (or Chermidae) is the Apple Sucker, *Psylla mali*, the nymph of which is very injurious to apple blossom. Species of aphids are also exceedingly common, such as the notorious Woolly Aphis, *Eriosoma lanigerum*, also known as American Blight.

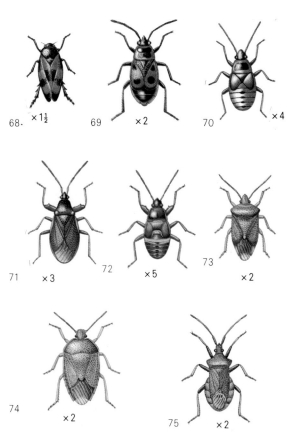

68. ×1½ 69 ×2 70 ×4

71 ×3 72 ×5 73 ×2

74 ×2 75 ×2

Land Bugs: **68** Froghopper, *Cercopis vulnerata*, **69** Red Bug, *Pyrrhocoris apterus*, **70** its nymph, **71** Pinecone Bug, *Gastrodes grossipes*, **72** its nymph, **73** Shield Bug, *Elasmostethus interstinctus*, **74** Shield Bug, *Piezodorus lituratus*, **75** Shield Bug, *Coreus marginatus*

79

It produces the white wool-like masses of sticky material found on fruit-trees. The Bean Aphis is *Aphis fabae*, also called Black Aphis, Black Blight, and many more names.

The scale-insects are included in the super-family Coccoidea. The Brown Scale is *Parthenolecanium corni*, which is common on fruit bushes and wild plants. The Mussel Scale is *Lepidosaphes ulmi*, the commonest of all scale insects, being particularly abundant in apple orchards. Its popular name is derived from its scales, which resemble miniature mussels.

The life-histories of pests belonging to other genera are similarly all extremely interesting to read about; they are explained in detail in larger text-books.

Sub-Order Heteroptera
(Order Hemiptera)

Whilst the eggs of the sub-order Homoptera are in general fairly simple in structure and ovoid in shape, those of the Heteroptera are, on the contrary, objects of much beauty as regards shape, sculpture and colouring. However, despite the diversity, they are constant in the different families, and may act as a guide to identification. There are also curious structural peculiarities on some eggs, such as filaments, a fringe of processes encircling an operculum (egg-cap) and so on.

From the egg emerges a nymph which develops, by gradual changes, into the adult. The insects may therefore be met at all stages of development, and

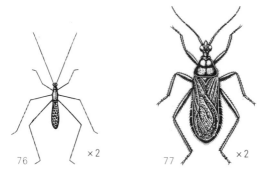

Assassin Bugs: **76** *Empicoris vagabundus,* **77** *Reduvius personatus*

some diversity of structure and colouring may bring about some confusion in identification. This may be seen from the examples illustrated. *Pyrrhocoris apterus* (**69**), the only British member of the family Pyrrhocoridae, the red bugs, is shown beside its nymph (**70**): the latter on attaining a length of 10 mm moults into its final form. A comparison between the imago of the Pinecone Bug, *Gastrodes grossipes* (**71**) and its nymph (**72**) illustrates a stage in the metamorphosis of a very common species. It lives chiefly on Scots Pine, the adults being found from the beginning of July to the beginning of August. *Acanthosoma haemorrhoidale,* found on hawthorn and other trees from August to October, belongs to the family Acanthosimadae, the shield bugs. This family and the Pentatomidae are noted for their beautiful colouring. They are also most interesting for the way in which

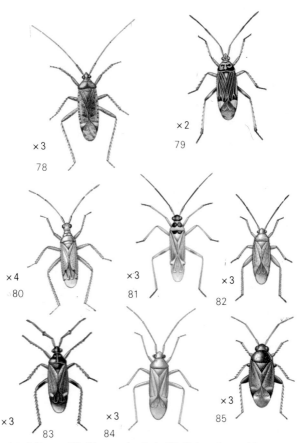

Land Bugs: **78** *Phytocoris ulmi*, **79** *Calocoris quadripunc-tatus*, **80** *Dicyphus epilobii*, **81** *Cyllecoris histrionicus*, **82** *Orthotylus ericetorum*, **83** *Harpocera thoracica*, **84** *Phylus coryli*, **85** *Psallus variabilis*

82

they care for their young, as in the common *Elasmostethus interstinctus* (**73**) which lives mainly on birch trees, as well as on other common British trees. The adult insect appears in August. One of the commonest shield bugs is *Piezodorus lituratus* (**74**) found on furze, where the whole of its life seems to be spent. *Coreus marginatus* (**75**) belongs to the family Coreidae, shield bugs which are narrower in shape than the related family of Pentatomidae, and which are able to emit more nauseous and penetrating odours than their close relations.

The assassin bugs belonging to the families Reduviidae and Nabidae form a very extensive family of aggressive carnivores. *Empicoris vagabundus* (**76**), hunts its living prey on the trunks of trees and furze, from July to October. From May to October *Reduvius personatus* (**77**) can be found. It is nocturnal and also frequents houses, where it attacks, among other insects, the Bed Bug, *Cimex lectularius* of the family Cimicidae. The latter is a pest of dirty houses; it lives behind wallpaper, in cracks, etc., and comes out in the dark to feed on blood from the exposed parts of the skin of sleeping people. The fore wings of all *Cimex* species have degenerated into mere pads, and there is no trace of a hind pair.

Many bugs are slender in shape. Such is the very common species *Phytocoris ulmi* (**78**) of the family Miridae, the adults being found from June to October on plants and trees. Other examples are *Calocoris quadripunctatus* (**79**) very common on oak from April to July, and *Dicyphus epilobii*

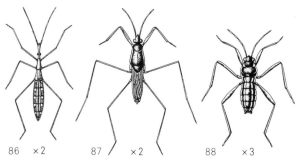

86 Water Measurer, *Hydrometra stagnorum*. **87** Pond Skater, *Gerris gibbifer*. **88** Water Cricket, *Velia caprai*

(80) found from July to October, and even later, on the Great Willow Herb, *Epilobium hirsutum*. It is a bug which appears to be more widely distributed here than abroad. *Cyllecoris histrionicus* (**81**) is also widely distributed, and found on oak from the middle of June to July, occasionally in August. It varies in colour. *Orthotylus ericetorum* (**82**) belongs to a genus of green bugs which escape notice because of the colour and small size, the largest measuring only 6·5 mm ($\frac{1}{4}$ in). This insect is, however, common from July to October on *Calluna vulgaris* (ling) and species of *Erica* (heaths). The common *Harpocera thoracica* (**83**) is found on hawthorn, oak, birch, hazel and sallow, from late May to June; it has distinctive antennae. Later, from June to August, we shall find *Phylus coryli* (**84**) on oak, as well as closely related *P. melanocephalus*. *Psallus variabilis* (**85**) varies much in colour, and is found from June to July on sallow and aspen. Not common.

84

The familiar insects known as pond skaters are bugs of the family Hydrometridae. The most noteworthy is the Water Measurer, *Hydrometra stagnorum*, (**86**) which walks in a leisurely manner over the surface of stagnant water and—like others of its kind—cannot get wet because of its light weight and its covering of fine hairs. *Gerris gibbifer* (**87**) is a member of the family Gerridae, the pond skaters, which unlike the previous species glide rapidly along the surface. Some species are wingless. The water crickets of the family Veliidae are smaller and congregate, often on slow streams. *Velia caprai* (**88**) is a common species. All these bugs, that move on the surface of the water but rarely if ever go down into the water, feed mainly on dead insects.

The true water bugs have their antennae hidden, a feature which gave rise to the name Cryptocerata, hidden horns. The absence of antennae immediately separates them from most water beetles (order Coleoptera) whose antennae are visible.

These true water bugs may be found in all stretches of water not chemically polluted by factories and the like, and quite stagnant water in the countryside and even in towns may be visited by them. They live submerged, and are not found on the surface, like the pond skaters, which belong to the antennae-visible group of Gymnocerata (pages 75–84). Water bugs occasionally fly from pond to pond. The eggs are laid on vegetation in water from which the young emerge and develop gradually into the adult form.

The Saucer Bug, *Ilyocoris cimicoides* (**89**) of the family Naucoridae, is quite a large and common

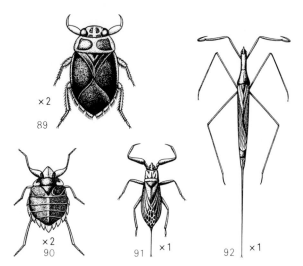

Water Bugs: **89** Saucer Bug, *Ilyocoris cimicoides*.
90 *Aphelocheirus montandoni*. **91** Water Scorpion, *Nepa cinerea*. **92** Water Scorpion, *Ranatra linearis*.

insect of still waters, where it lives among the weeds. Somewhat smaller and brighter in colour is *Aphelocheirus montandoni* (= *aestivalis*) a fast swimmer in stony rivers; perhaps due to this it is not easily found, though it appears to be quite plentiful when discovered. A most extraordinary water-dweller is *Ranatra linearis* (**92**), a water scorpion (family Nepidae), whose first pair of legs are modified for seizing prey, and are quite useless for walking, so that this insect appears to have only four legs. Our other water scorpion is *Nepa cinerea* (**91**). It is the more common of these two British

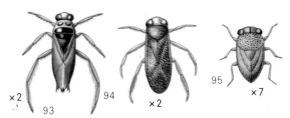

Water Bugs: **93** *Notonecta glauca*, **94** Water Boatman, *Corixa punctata*, **95** *Plea atomaria*

species, and it looks like a dead leaf. Its abdominal appendages shown in the illustrations are for breathing, and are not stings. Victims are held by the raptorial fore legs whilst the juices are sucked. The eggs of *Nepa* are laid individually in the stems and leaves of water plants. Many aquatic insects lay their eggs inside plant stems. The female of the common *Notonecta glauca* (**93**) has an ovipositor or egg-placer for this purpose. Notonectids can inflict painful bites, and are aggressive destroyers of tadpoles, small fish, etc. They are noted for swimming upside down, unlike the related family of Corixidae, such as *Corixa punctata* (**94**) and *Sigara dorsalis* which do not have this curious notonectid habit. Their legs are hairy, adapted for swimming, the third pair being particularly powerful and conspicuous, and give the impression of being oars attached to a tiny boat; hence the insects are popularly known as water boatmen. Not all species have the legs developed in this manner, however; for instance the small bug *Plea atomaria* (**95**) only crawls slowly about duckweed and other vegetation.

Description. Minute insects. Body slender, length 1–3 mm. Piercing mouthparts. Antennae 6- to 9-jointed. Wingless or with very narrow wings fringed with hairs. Metamorphosis incomplete. Colour mostly black or yellow.

Classification. Two sub-orders, the *TEREBRANTIA*, having a saw-like ovipositor and at least one longitudinal vein in the fore wings, and the *TUBULIFERA*, having no ovipositor and hardly any venation in the wings. (About 183 British species.)

Thrips or thunder flies live on flowers, among foliage, in decaying plants, wood and fungi. Some are predatory and attack aphids, but the majority of them feed on plants, and because of their numbers they can become serious economic pests. The worst of these are the onion thrips, the turnip thrips and the bean thrips. Other thrip pests attack pears, grasses, etc., and infest greenhouses. Thrips cause major problems for fire services, since they are small enough to penetrate and activate smoke alarms.

In some species males are rare and eggs are able to develop parthenogenetically (without fertilization).

Division (b), *ENDOPTERYGOTA*
Insects with wings developing internally

The most highly evolved insects belong to the *ENDOPTERYGOTA* (see page 45). Their larvae reveal no external evidence of the future winged insects into which they will eventually be transformed.

The complete metamorphosis undergone by these insects—from the egg, via the larva and eventually from pupa to adult—is unique in the animal kingdom. It enables the larva to be specialized for rapid growth, and the adult to be specialized for reproduction; incidentally providing a fascinating opportunity for sustained observation.

ALDERFLIES, SNAKEFLIES, LACEWINGS
Order Neuroptera

Description. Body soft. Antennae long. Mouthparts adapted for biting. Four similar membranous wings, held roof-wise when at rest. Larvae carnivorous with mouthparts adapted for biting or sucking. Includes aquatic larvae.

Classification. Two sub-orders, the MEGALOPTERA, alderflies and snakeflies, usually having no marked forking of the branches of the veins near the margins of the wings, larvae with biting mouthparts, and the PLANIPENNIA, lacewings, etc., usually having the branches of the veins markedly forked at the margins of the wings, larvae with mouthparts adapted for sucking. There are over 60 British species of Neuroptera.

This order comprises weak-flying insects. They possess much diversity of form, and their life-histories are just as varied. Individuals are not found in large numbers, but they are by no means uncommon. The larvae, all carnivorous feeders, are particularly curious in structure, especially so in the case of the aquatic forms.

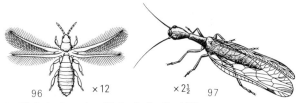

96 $\times 12$ $\times 2\frac{1}{2}$ 97

96 Thrip (1–3 mm), **97** Snakefly, *Raphidia notata*

89

It has been suggested that alderflies and snakeflies should be separated into two distinct orders because these insects differ in many respects from each other. The reasons are of no concern to us here, where we need but consider a few of the common species. Alderflies (family Sialidae), such as *Sialis lutaria* (**98**) lay their eggs on plants and objects close to the edge of the water. One female will lay as many as 200 to 700 greyish eggs, kept together in one mass. On hatching, the larvae make their way to the water, where they may be found in the mud of ponds and slow-moving streams. The larvae are carnivorous and have well-developed jaws for seizing other larvae, worms, and so on. They have complicated lateral processes, often jointed, attached to the abdominal segments;

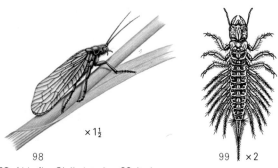

×1½

98   99 ×2

98 Alderfly, *Sialis lutaria*. **99** its larva

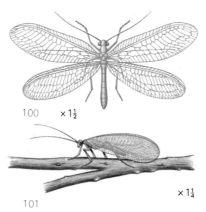

100 ×1½

101 ×1¼

Green Lacewing, *Chrysopa carnea:* **100** set. **101** at rest

these are breathing gills. The larva of *Sialis lutaria* with these processes is shown (**99**). The larvae leave the water when fully grown and burrow into the soil, where they pupate.

The snakeflies, family Raphidiidae, with three British species, are found in woods, on hawthorn when in blossom, and other flowers. They are, however, not common. *Raphidia notata* (**97**) is illustrated as an example of the unusual appearance of these insects, making them easily recognizable and demonstrating the origin—as in the case of scorpion-flies—of their popular English name. The eggs are inserted by means of an ovipositor into openings in bark. The larvae live mainly under loose bark; they are very voracious predators of soft-bodied insects.

Varied as this group of insects is, their larvae nevertheless bear a greater resemblance to each other than do the adult insects, these—especially foreign species—being often very different in form. All larvae have piercing and sucking mouth parts, and are carnivorous feeders.

British species, however, may be referred to as lacewings, so named after their relatively large, transparent, gauze-like wings, which are held roof-wise over the body when at rest. Large wings, in relation to the size of the body, are rarely attributes of fast fliers, and indeed the flight of lacewings is a leisurely, gentle business which would be a highly dangerous undertaking if they were not crepuscular and nocturnal in habit.

The commonest of these insects are the green lacewings (family Chrysopidae), especially *Chrysopa carnea* (**100** set, **101** at rest), which comes inside houses and other buildings to hibernate. This species is remarkable in that it loses its green colour during the over-wintering period, when it is reddish, but it regains its characteristic pale green in the spring. The eggs are attached to the underside of leaves and are borne on stalk-like threads, so that they are protectively raised away from the leaf (**102**). Lacewing larvae have the features of larval predators, well-developed eyes, useful jaws, and legs that give them freedom of movement. They feed especially on plant-lice of all kinds, and are most helpful to gardeners. Some species attach debris to their bodies. When ready to

×5

102 Eggs of Lacewing

pupate, the larvae spin hard cocoons of white silk on leaves and other suitable supports. Unlike most insect larvae, they produce their silk in transformed abdominal organs (Malpighian tubes), and it comes out of an anal spinneret.

The adults are sometimes known as Golden Eyes, from the bright lustre to be seen in their large compound eyes. Other species are also called Stink-flies because when handled they are able to emit a disagreeable smell from glands situated in the thorax.

There are also smaller species of sombre colour known as brown lacewings (family Hemerobiidae). They are much more delicate in appearance than the green lacewings, and they do not raise their eggs from the surface to which they are attached. The larvae also feed on aphids.

The largest member of this order of Neuroptera belongs to the family Osmylidae; it is *Osmylus*

103 Lacewing, *Osmylus fulvicephalus*   × 1½

fulvicephalus (**103** with wings 'set'), found from May to July in dense vegetation beside clear streams. This species too does not raise its eggs on stalks. The larvae hatch about July and are amphibious. They live in mosses, and will go into water in search of small larvae, particularly those of flies. Pupation, in cocoons, takes place in April and May.

SCORPION FLIES Order Mecoptera

Description. Slender carnivorous insects. Head beaklike. Antennae long and thin. Long, slender legs. Four similar membranous wings, held lengthwise and horizontally when at rest. Larvae carnivorous, having three pairs of thoracic legs. Metamorphosis complete.

Classification. A well-defined order divided into families with three hundred species. (4 British species.)

The popular name for this insect is derived from the easily recognized male, which has the last abdominal segments curved upwards; it reminds one of a scorpion. Another very distinctive feature is the beak-like head, such as that of *Panorpa communis* (**104**) which greatly helps in the identification of these insects. They are carnivorous at all stages of their lives, but they seem to prefer dead or injured insects. Scorpion flies live in shady and damp vegetation. The caterpillar-like larvae pupate in the soil. The pupa is capable of movement when disturbed, and apparently makes its way to the surface when the adult is about to emerge.

BUTTERFLIES AND MOTHS Order Lepidoptera

Description. Four membranous wings. Few crossveins. Body, wings and appendages covered with broad scales. Principal mouthparts generally a suctorial proboscis formed by the maxillae. Metamorphosis complete. Some larvae have eight pairs of limbs.

Classification. It has been the custom to divide the LEPIDOPTERA into RHOPALOCERA (butterflies, in the British species always with clubbed antennae) and HETEROCERA (moths, antennae very varied). There are however, objections to such divisions, as there are also objections to the familiar amateur divisions of MACRO- and MICROLEPIDOPTERA, based on size criteria. Scientifically the Lepidoptera were classed in two suborders, the HOMONEURA, having the venation of the fore and hind wings almost identical, and the HETERONEURA, with venation of the fore and hind wings markedly different. The HETERONEURA comprised the vast majority of the Lepidoptera. Of recent years studies and comparisons with species from all over the world have

104 Scorpion Fly, *Panorpa communis*   × 1½

made systematists abandon the various groupings mentioned; there is in fact no natural division that justifies separating butterflies from moths—that is, of course, from the purely scientific point of view. Doing away with the two great divisions may seem strange to British lepidopterists who are well aware of the marked differences between the butterflies and moths found in the British Isles. The former are daylight creatures which flourish in the sun; the numerous moths are of the night—but, paradoxically, there are, nevertheless, beautiful daytime fliers too. There are even some moths with butterfly-like antennae. (2,200 British species.)

For convenience we may here continue to divide the Lepidoptera into two groups, Rhopalocera and Heterocera, generally referred to as butterflies and moths. These insects, with the exception of a few wingless female moths, all have four wings, covered in minute overlapping scales which are easily rubbed off. All butterflies, and most moths, have mouthparts in the shape of a long tongue, adapted for sucking nectar from flowers, but a few moths are unable to feed at all in the imago stage.

The main distinction between British butterflies and moths lies in the antennae. In butterflies these organs are narrow with a club-shaped tip. In moths they vary very much and are sometimes large and feathery, sometimes thin and thread-like, rarely clubbed, the Burnets (*Zygaena*) being the one exception.

A typical butterfly or moth caterpillar has eight pairs of legs, three jointed pairs with small claws on the thorax or fore body and five pairs of short fleshy abdominal feet which are used for grasping the food-plant on which it sits.

Butterfly chrysalids (pupae) vary greatly in shape

and colour, and are sometimes covered with sharp spines. They are frequently attached to a support by a small pad of silk and a silken girdle—such as that of the Orange-tip—but are never enclosed in a cocoon. The pupae of moths are usually brown in colour, fairly smooth and protected by some kind of cocoon made from particles of soil, chewed wood or debris bound together with silk. Sometimes the pupa lies in a chamber hollowed out in the earth.

Life-history of Lepidoptera

The egg. All life begins with a fertilized egg. The eggs of the varied lepidopterous species differ much in appearance from each other when seen with the aid of a powerful magnifying glass or with a microscope (preferably a stereoscopic one). In shape some are elongate and this type will be found on a leaf where the female attached them standing

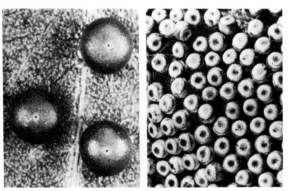

105 Eggs of Puss Moth, *Cerura vinula* × 10, **106** eggs of Vapourer Moth, *Orgyia antiqua* × 10

on end. They are normally on the underside of a leaf. Eggs are laid, or rather glued in position, either singly or in batches. Like the adults to come, the eggs are objects of great beauty. They are regular in form and many have attractive colours and markings on the surface: during the heyday of microscopy they were objects of popular study. Mounted specimens for the microscope may be obtained from instrument dealers.

Caterpillars. The leaf-eating larvae of butterflies are normally called caterpillars; woodborers and other types of feeders are usually referred to as larvae, or grubs when very small. On hatching, the tiny larva eats the egg shell as its first meal, though not all species do this. Then the serious business of growing becomes the all-absorbing task. It is a voracious eater of the first order. It is quite fascinating to watch a leaf-eater, hard at work. The leaf is held by the thoracic legs (situated on the first three segments of the body,

107 Larva of Cream-spot Tiger Moth, *Arctia villica* × 1

108 Larva of Silver-washed Fritillary. *Argynnis paphia* ×2

they are the true legs), the head is held as high as it can reach, then with a scything motion downwards as far as it can go, the caterpillar slices off a part of the leaf, then up goes the head again, and so the scything goes on and on. The abdominal prolegs hold the caterpillar firmly on its support, and serve also for locomotion; they disappear with the end of the larval stage.

The caterpillars feed on the plants where the eggs were laid. Each goes about its business; however, the larvae of some species are gregarious and have a sociable disposition. The Lackey moth, *Malacosoma neustria*, caterpillars hatch in April from eggs laid the previous year and immediately start making a 'tent' which is strong and waterproof, even bird-proof. Here they shelter, moult in safety, and at times sunbathe outside. Another example of a tent builder is the Ermine moth, *Spilosoma lubricipeda*, whose small caterpillars are more numerous than those of the Lackey so that the tents will be found to be even larger. It is a surprising

109 Larva of Pebble Prominent Moth, *Notodonta ziczac*

sight to see the hectic activity caused when tearing open one of these shelters.

The chitin which forms the larval skin does not grow, so at regular intervals the caterpillar, as it increases in size has to shed its skin, i.e., it has to moult. This is accomplished by the splitting of the skin which then falls away. This moulting occurs three or more times. The larva when fully grown becomes sluggish and prepares to pupate on its food plant or seeks shelter elsewhere according to the habits of its species.

The chrysalis or pupa. The caterpillar metamorphoses (transforms) into a pupa, which is often termed a chrysalis, particularly when referring to those of butterflies. This involves considerable preparation on the part of the larva. Some, like the Orange-tip butterfly, *Anthocharis cardamines* (**110**), make a silken pad on which to rest and also make a girdle round the waist. Many others (e.g. among the Fritillaries) suspend themselves by a hook which they make and so hang upside down; this we can ascertain because at the pupal stage we can now see many parts of the adult insect's anatomy, the

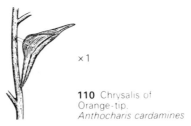

×1

110 Chrysalis of Orange-tip. *Anthocharis cardamines*

undeveloped wings and mouthparts are well in evidence. The pupal stage of all Lepidoptera reveals this.

Now a resting period intervenes: the pupae are, in Shelley's words '... an antenatal tomb, where butterflies dream of the life to come'. Other species of Lepidoptera, mostly moths, make cocoons or go below the surface of the ground and pupate without making any sort of protective covering for themselves. They are referred to as 'free' pupae, and are also found among butterflies. The common Grayling, *Hipparchia semele*, is one. Cocoons on the bark of trees, such as the one made by the common Puss Moth, *Cerura vinula*, which is made of chewed-up wood, become exceedingly hard so that in the spring when the moth emerges it secretes from the mouth potassium hydroxide to soften the cocoon, otherwise it would be unable to get out. It is further assisted by having a 'scraper' (part of its mouthparts) and because some of the pupal skin remains in position to protect the eyes and part of the head; it falls away when the moth is out of the cocoon. This happens in May or June. Pupation took place in August or September of the previous year.

The imago, or adult eventually, according to the time of the year and the species, emerges and climbs up to a suitable place. There it waits until a fluid is pumped into the sagging wings which then rapidly expand and harden, exposing at last the amazing colours and patterning for which the numerous members of this order are so justly renowned. It can now fly away and mate, and the life cycle is complete.

Mostly emergence occurs during the more clement months of the year when there is an assured food supply, many species being dependent on deciduous plants. However, the wonders of nature never cease for emergence happens even in mid-winter. One example, appropriately named the

×1

111

×1

112

Butterflies: **111** Clouded Yellow, *Colias croceus*, **112** Painted Lady, *Cynthia cardui*

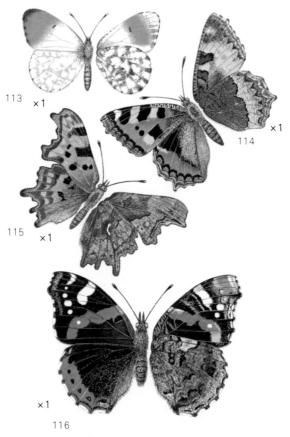

Butterflies: **113** Orange-tip, *Anthocharis cardamines*,
114 Small Tortoiseshell, *Aglais urticae*, **115** Comma,
Polygonia c-album, **116** Red Admiral, *Vanessa atalanta*

Winter Moth, *Operophtera brumata*, is widely distributed and will be found in the winter until late February. It is a serious pest of fruit trees. Orchard owners place sticky bands round the trunks of the trees to prevent the female from climbing up to lay her eggs in crevices and unopened buds. The female cannot fly.

RHOPALOCERA. *Butterflies*

Our appreciation of butterflies is universal. A butterfly is a flower that flies. A flower is a fixed butterfly. It is essentially a creature of summer sunshine. Its beauty ensured that it would be the first of the insect legion to attract the attention of early enquirers and so emerged the true lepidopterists, the first entomologists. It is not surprising therefore that as a result of their enthusiasm a voluminous literature has come into being, which is constantly being added to; so the specialized books can be readily consulted for every detail. Here we can look but briefly into the lore of the Lepidoptera, a wonderful order that whets one's interest to know more; there are thousands of them.

PIERIDAE, *the Whites and Yellows*. Some are very well known. There is for instance the famous—or should we say infamous?—Large White, *Pieris brassicae*, one of the insects that attracted early scientific interest; it was already described more than three hundred years ago. Its caterpillar is a pest of cabbage fields where it can cause enormous destruction. Emergence is from eggs laid in batches, and there are two broods in one year; furthermore it is an immigrant in autumn from the

Baltic region. It can be exceedingly abundant and at other times scarce due to weather conditions, predators and parasitic Hymenoptera, especially the ichneumon *Apanteles glomaratus*. This butterfly is widely distributed here and abroad. It is on the wing from April till June, the second brood from July to September, and there may be even a further generation. Of the same genus is the ubiquitous Small White, *Pieris rapae*, also a migrant; its larva feeds on cabbage and related plants such as nasturtium and mignonette. Eggs are laid singly on the underside of leaves. Both the Whites have two broods in the year, the second differing from the first in that the blackish tips and spots are darker. A more attractive member of the family is the Orange-tip, *Anthocharis cardamines*, (**113**), common in May and June. It is associated with several species of plants especially those of the hedgerows. The young larvae are cannibalistic. Another pierid found in similar places and in the rides of woods is the Brimstone *Gonepteryx rhamni* (**117**); the food-plant is buckthorn. A family relation of it is the beautiful Clouded Yellow, *Colias croceus* (**111**), on the wing in August and September in clover and lucerne fields. Sometimes it is scarce, but at other times it can be very numerous—a description that applies to this species as it does to six of our nine pierid immigrants. In the case of the Clouded Yellow they come from Spain and North Africa.

NYMPHALIDAE, *the Brush-footed Butterflies.* Several species of this large family have dense tufts of scales on the forelegs, which do not function as legs. Nymphalids are distributed all round the

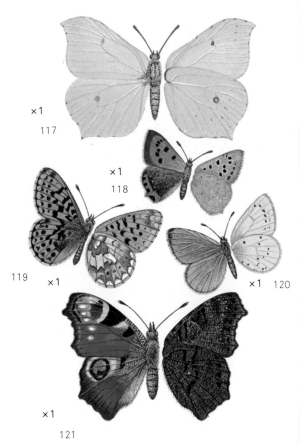

×1

117

×1

118

119 ×1

×1 120

×1

121

Butterflies: **117** Brimstone, *Gonepteryx rhamni*, **118** Small Copper, *Lycaena phlaeas*, **119** Pearl-bordered Fritillary, *Boloria (Clossiana) euphrosyne*, **120** Holly Blue, *Celastrina argiolus*, **121** Peacock, *Inachis io*

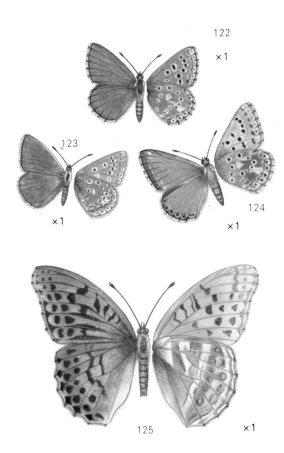

Butterflies: **122** Adonis Blue, *Lysandra bellargus*,
123 Common Blue, *Polyommatus icarus*, **124** Chalk Hill
Blue, *Lysandra coridon*, **125** Silver-washed Fritillary,
Argynnis (Argynnis) paphia

world and include some very handsome members. Some of the British listed species are migrants. One is the Painted Lady, *Cynthia cardui* (**112**) and there is also the well known Red Admiral, *Vanessa atalanta* (**116**). Its caterpillars are a common sight on stinging nettles, and hops. It is widely distributed but only occasionally hibernates in Britain. Its immigrants come from the Mediterranean region. It will be found visiting flowers, especially those of *Buddleia* which are popular with many insects. This butterfly is on the wing from May and June till October. Also from larvae that feed on nettle we get the Peacock, *Inachis io* (**121**) in August and September. It hibernates in hollow tree trunks and similar shelter. During the same late summer period will be seen the attractive Small Tortoiseshell, *Aglais urticae* (**114**); it is of the second brood because those of the first were on the wing in June. Its foodplant is nettle as it is also of the Comma, *Polygonia c-album* (**115**); the larva also feeds on hops. The Comma visits flowers and fallen fruit. The butterfly is remarkable for the irregular contour of the wings; they make for perfect camouflage when at rest.

A number of species resemble each other. Two of several illustrate this: the Pearl-bordered Fritillary, *Boloria* (*Clossiana*) *euphrosyne* (**119**) on the wing in May and June, and the Silver-washed Fritillary, *Argynnis paphia* (**125**); both were formerly numerous, but have declined in numbers and distribution in recent years.

LYCAENIDAE, *the Hairstreaks, Coppers and Blues*. All are small, often brilliantly coloured. Their

126 Larva of Lobster Moth, *Stauropus fagi* × 1½,
127 Lobster Moth × 1½

caterpillars resemble woodlice. Large Blue *Maculinea arion* caterpillars fall to the ground after the third moult. They are taken for 'milking' of their 'honey' glands by ants. They became extinct in Britain in 1979, but were reintroduced in 1983.

The Small Copper, *Lycaena phlaeas* (**118**) which hibernates as a larva, is very common, chiefly in May, July and early August, and in October. The chrysalids of some lycaenids stridulate, such as that of the Small Copper.

The Adonis Blue, *Lysandra bellargus* (**122**) in mid-May to mid-June will be found flying together with the Common Blue, *Polyommatus icarus* (**123**) as well as the Chalk Hill Blue, *Lysandra coridon* (**124**). The females of several Blues are darker coloured. The Holly Blue, *Celastrina argiolus* (**120**), is on the wing from April till May, the second brood in July and August. The first brood feeds on holly; the eggs for the second brood are laid on the flowering shoots of ivy. The imagines have been seen feeding on dung, carrion, and the sap of trees.

The vast majority of our Lepidoptera are moths. Most of them are nocturnal, although some fly by day and are gaily coloured; these are usually mistaken for butterflies. The antennae are very varied—not clubbed—with the exception of the British Burnets (*Zygaena*, a genus of the family Zygaenidae); theirs gradually thicken distally and so look club-like. The few moths mentioned below illustrate some of the better known of our species, the first a pest!

YPONOMEUTIDAE. This family must be mentioned in this survey of our numerous insects because of a small, inconspicuous moth, *Plutella xylostella*, known in the British Isles as the Diamond Back Moth. It is probably the most widely spread of all the Lepidoptera in the world, notorious because it is a serious pest of cabbage and related plants of economic importance, such as cauliflower and other Cruciferae. It is a migrant, invading at times in large numbers the East Coast, coming from Northern Europe and Scandinavia. Eggs are laid singly. The caterpillar grows to only

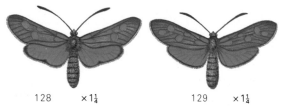

128 ×1¼   129 ×1¼

Moths: **128** Five-spot Burnet, *Zygaena trifolii*, **129** Six-spot Burnet, *Zygaena filipendulae*

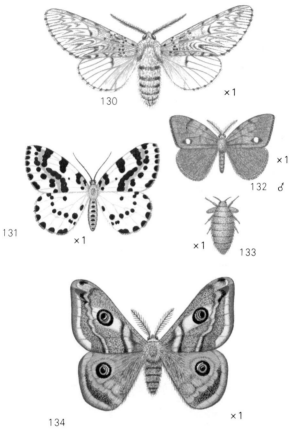

130 ×1

131 ×1

132 ♂ ×1

133 ×1

134 ×1

Moths: **130** Puss Moth, *Cerura vinula*, **131** Magpie,
Abraxas grossulariata, **132** Vapourer, *Orgyia antiqua*, male,
133 Vapourer, female, **134** Emperor, *Saturnia pavonia*

8 mm long, and the imago 11–15 mm. As a pest it is the rival of the White butterflies.

ZYGAENIDAE, *Burnets*. They live in colonies and fly by day; their bright colours warn predators that they are distasteful. In sunshine they look like butterflies, their club-like antennae adding to the deception. The females have stouter bodies than the males. The larvae make paper-like cocoons on the stems of plants. The Five-spot Burnet, *Zygaena trifolii* (128), which may take two years to complete its life cycle, occurs, as its name implies, on bird's-foot trefoil, and also on clover. It is on the wing in May and June. The Six-spot Burnet, *Z. filipendulae* (129), unlike the Five-spot, is not local in range but common in many parts of the country in July and August in sunny weather. The caterpillar feeds in autumn, hibernates, and continues its development in the spring.

SATURNIIDAE includes but one British species, the diurnal (day-flying) Emperor Moth, *Pavonia pavonia* (134), to be seen in April and May on heaths

135 Larva of Old Lady Moth, *Mormo maura* × 1¼

136 Larva of Emperor Moth, *Pavonia pavonia* × 1¼

and moors and along estuaries. It flies during warm, sunny weather in the afternoon. Foodplant: ling, bramble and blackthorn.

GEOMETRIDAE is the large family to which the Winter Moth, already mentioned, belongs. Another is the Magpie Moth, *Abraxas grossulariata* (**131**), also called the Currant Moth, for its caterpillar is a pest on fruit bushes and trees in May and June; elm is also one of its foods. There is much variation in colour patterning of this beautiful but warningly-coloured moth. On the wing in July and August, it flies slowly when disturbed. The larvae at rest look remarkably like twigs; another peculiarity is that they have one pair only of prolegs, here called claspers. When moving, they arch the body, forming loops as they progress, so they are called "loopers", or "geometers" as they seem to measure the ground, hence the name Geometridae.

SPHINGIDAE, the Hawk Moths, are spectacular members of our insect fauna because of their size, attractive colour patterning, and their remarkable flying powers. Some are said to be able to fly at 36

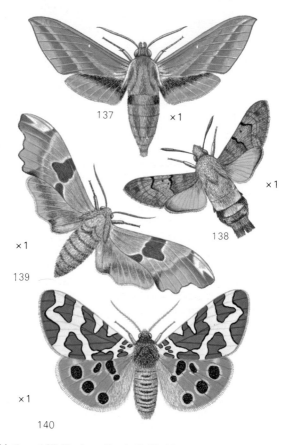

Moths: **137** Elephant Hawk, *Deilephila elpenor*,
138 Humming-bird Hawk, *Macroglossum stellatarum*,
139 Lime Hawk, *Mimas tiliae*, **140** Garden Tiger, *Arctia caja*

×1

141 Cinnabar Moth, *Tyria jacobaeae*

miles per hour; others can hover like bees and can have partly transparent wings—the Bee Hawk Moths, *Hemaris fuciformis* and *H. tityus*, which are on the wing in May. To attain a speed of 36 mph the moth has to exert 70 wing beats per second (*cf.* Mosquito, 300 wing beats for only 2 mph; the White butterfly, 12 for 6 mph).

The caterpillars of this family are large and possess an upright hook at the end of the body on the eighth segment, a distinctive feature. The chrysalids lie buried in the ground.

The commonest of these nocturnal species is the Privet Hawk Moth, *Sphinx ligustri*, found in June; it breeds here and is also replenished by immigrants. Its cocoon is not strongly made; nevertheless the pupal stage lasts some nine months and may even continue for three years. The Lime Hawk, *Mimas tiliae* (**139**) is one of the most handsome of our seventeen species; it flies at night early in May, the month when so many of these moths are active. There is considerable variation in colour in this species; at rest it is difficult to detect. Its beauty is surpassed by that of the Elephant Hawks, *Deilephila elpenor* (**137**), and the smaller *D. porcellus*. Except for the difference in size the two resemble each other. The caterpillars hide in the daytime low down among the herbage but at night they climb up to feed on willow herb, fuchsia, virginia creeper and other plants. The larva of the smaller species, however, feeds mainly at night on bedstraw. These two Elephant Hawks are closely related; hybrids have been noted and are fertile.

Another remarkably strong flier of this family is the Humming-bird Hawk, *Macroglossum stellatarum* (**138**); like the Bee Hawks, this species is a day flier and loves sunshine. It visits blossoms hovering in front of them while inserting its long proboscis to feed on the nectar. It is an annual immigrant in spring from the Mediterranean region. The caterpillar and eggs laid here feed on bedstraw and do so in the daytime as well as at night.

ARCTIIDAE, *Tiger and Ermine Moths, etc*. We have forty species of this large family of which two may be mentioned as they are well known. The familiar 'woolly bear' caterpillars belong to it. The Garden Tiger moth, *Arctia caja* (**140**), is one of the beautiful species; the colour patterning is subject to much variation. The Garden Tiger exemplifies the general aspect of these thick-bodied moths. This one is on the wing in July, occasionally in August. The colours are of the warning type and as these species are most unpalatable, predators learn to leave them well alone. Much more so is the Cinnabar Moth, *Tyria jacobaeae* (**141**), which is the only member of its genus and is restricted to Europe. It is also garishly coloured. The Cinnabar may be seen flying in a leisurely way by day at the end of May and in June. Its black and yellow banded caterpillars are familiar on ragwort in July and August.

LYMANTRIIDAE, *Tussock Moths*. The common Vapourer moth or Rusty Tussock, *Orgyia antiqua* (**132-3**), is a common species in which the female is wingless—the wings are reduced to mere stumps. She remains at the cocoon from which she emerged and the day-flying winged male finds her there in June. The eggs are laid on the cocoon and hatch the following spring. This species feeds on a variety of plants and trees. There are two generations in a year.

CADDIS FLIES Order Trichoptera

Description. Moth-like insects. Mouthparts appear vestigial or absent. Antennae bristly. Wings membranous and hairy, held roof-wise when at rest. Much venation but few cross-veins. Larvae aquatic, usually living in cases.
Classification. The order is divided into families only. (193 British species.)

The order is a large one; over 3,000 species have so far been scientifically described. Nearly all pass the immature states of their lives in water, as do mayflies.

Aquatic insects. Caddis flies belong to a more evolved order, and it is perhaps useful to take the opportunity of referring here to all aquatic insects. In the British Isles eleven orders out of twenty-nine have members that live in water at some stage of their development, or for nearly the whole of their adult lives; some never quit water unless forced to do so. The eleven orders are the Collembola (springtails), Ephemeroptera (mayflies), Odonata (dragonflies), Plecoptera (stoneflies), Hemiptera (bugs), Neuroptera (alder flies), Coleoptera (beetles), Trichoptera (caddis flies), Lepidoptera (butterflies and moths), Diptera (true flies), and Hymenoptera (ichneumon flies etc.). However, insects are essentially terrestrial animals and they have to breathe air. Most cannot extract oxygen from water, though the nymphal (larval) stage of many species can.

The imagines (adults) that remain and live in water must come up to breathe or to get air at the surface. Few adults live in water, and these are either beetles or bugs. They, as well as those that live on the surface of the water, have evolved anatomical adaptations to suit this type of life. Oarshaped legs for quick movement in a dense medium are one example. The larvae possess means of breathing dissolved oxygen from the water.

Trichoptera. The name caddis fly continues to puzzle entomologists. How did the name originate? Shakespeare calls it the caddis man. These insects are mostly nocturnal and are thus little seen. They are readily attracted to lights and this can result in thousands of them being found dead round lakeside lamps. They can travel quite long distances and are thus able to repopulate ponds that have dried up. Their presence indicates really fresh water. Caddis flies can be confused with dull coloured moths, but instead of scales they are clothed with dense hairs; furthermore they have no curled-up proboscis. The imagines are often said not to feed, because of the

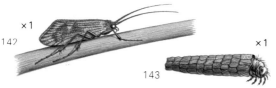

×1

142

×1

143

142 Caddis Fly, *Phryganea grandis.* **143** its larva

absence of suitable mouthparts. Many do feed, using a protrusible haustellum never seen in museum specimens because it is retracted and visible only in living caddises. Some probably do not feed. When at rest they fold their wings like a tent over their backs.

The eggs are laid in or near water. The aquatic larvae breathe by gills. There are very few species that are terrestrial; one is British: *Enoicyla pusilla*, apparently found only in Worcestershire in late autumn and early winter. The female is wingless. It occurs on oak leaves eating the epidermal layer.

One of our two large caddis flies, common in May to July, is *Phryganea grandis* (**142**). It has a wingspan of 6·5 cm. As in most of these insects the larva makes a case to protect its soft body, in this species, from vegetable material. The larva is omnivorous and will even attack small fish. There is considerable variety in caddis cases depending on the species, but some do not make any. Trout are known to blow out caddis larvae from their cases and then catch them for food; they are also known to suck out the cases.

Fly fishermen use the larvae and the adults as lures, calling them 'sedges'; *Phryganea grandis* is their 'great red sedge'.

Description. Two membranous wings, the hind pair modified into halteres or balancers. Mouthparts adapted for sucking, sometimes for piercing. Segments of thorax fused. Metamorphosis complete.

Classification. There are three sub-orders, this being particularly evinced by the larval and pupal stages; the NEMATOCERA, larvae well developed, head free or projected, horizontally biting mandibles, antennae of imago (adult) longer than head and thorax and many-jointed; BRACHYCERA, larvae with incompletely developed head which can be withdrawn within the body, antennae of imago shorter than thorax, very variable and having usually 3 joints, the last long; the CYCLORRHAPHA, head of the larva only a relic, antennae of imago 3-jointed. There are about 6,500 British Diptera.

An entomologist does not use the word 'fly' indiscriminately, for to him it refers only to the two-winged insects of the Diptera. The order is extensive, comprising insects which are mainly active in daylight, especially in sunshine. They visit flowers for nectar, or decaying animal or plant

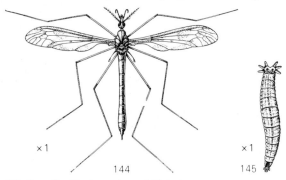

×1   ×1

144   145

144 Cranefly, *Tipula maxima*, **145** its larva

refuse; others are predatory on insects, whilst the females of many species are blood-suckers of animals and birds. The feeding habits make many of them dangerous carriers or transmitters of disease. The vectors of malaria, yellow fever and sleeping sickness are species of Diptera. The following tabulation gives the popular names of a selection of flies, and shows how the families are arranged in the classification of the order.

TWO-WINGED FLIES

Sub-Order NEMATOCERA

Tipulidae	Crane-flies or Daddy-long-legs
Culicidae	Mosquitoes, Gnats
Cecidomyiidae	Gall-midges
Mycetophilidae	Fungus-gnats
Chironomidae	Midges

Sub-Order BRACHYCERA

Stratiomyidae	Soldier-flies
Tabanidae	Clegs, Horse-flies, Gad-flies
Asilidae	Robber-flies
Bombyliidae	Bee-flies

Sub-Order CYCLORRHAPHA

Syrphidae	Hover-flies
Conopidae	Thick-headed Flies
Braulidae	Bee-lice
Tachinidae (Larvaevoridae)	Parasitic-flies
Calliphoridae	Bluebottles, Greenbottles, Blow-flies
Oestridae	Warble- or Bot-flies
Muscidae	House-flies, Stable-flies
Hippoboscidae	Forest-flies, Sheep-keds
Nycteribiidae	Parasites on Bats

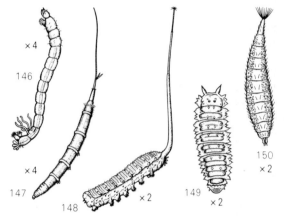

Larvae of Diptera: **146** *Chironomus* (Bloodworm).
147 *Ptychoptera*, **148** Rat-tailed Maggot, *Eristalis*.
149 Syrphid, **150** *Stratiomys*

The Larvae of Diptera. The habits of larvae often excite more curiosity than do the other stages of an insect's life-history, even when it is a species in which complete metamorphosis exists. Flies have a greater diversity of larval habits than is to be observed in any other order, and we have seen how the structure of larvae differs according to the sub-order. Some of them are plant feeders, often are very destructive pests; others are useful scavengers, feeding on rotting animal and vegetable matter. Many larvae are useful parasites, checking the increase of other insects, though among these larvae are also harmful parasites of mammals, including man. The specialized morphological adaptation to their surroundings may be seen from examination of the larva of a Crane-fly which feeds on roots. It is the gardener's Leatherjacket, having a hard skin and a distinct head, provided with biting mouth-parts and antennae. The larva of our largest Crane-fly, *Tipula maxima* (imago—**144,** larva—**145**) lives in wet banks of ponds and streams; the lobes at the posterior end are for breathing. Similar structures in the aquatic 'Bloodworm' larvae of *Chironomus* (**146**) are, however, not for respiration. This larva also has pseudopods (false legs), close to the small head as well as on the last abdominal segment.

The larvae of the family Ptychopteridae live in shallow water in mud and debris, breathing being assured by a long 'tail', held upwards (**147**). A similar projection to enable easy respiration may be seen in a syrphid larva, the Rat-tailed Maggot (**148**). The *Stratiomys* larva (**150**) has a row of hairs to buoy it up at the surface of the water so as to leave the anal spiracles (breathing holes) exposed to the air.

The larvae of culicine mosquitoes, for example *Culex* (**151**), breathe through a tube protruded at intervals above the surface of the water. The larvae of anopheline mosquitoes, *Anopheles* (**152**), breathe

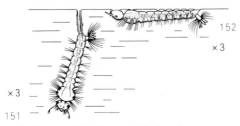

Mosquito larvae: **151** *Culex.* **152** *Anopheles*

Mosquitoes: **153** *Culex,* **154** *Anopheles*

through spiracles on the eighth abdominal segment, which is held against the surface-film. Control of these insects is effected by spraying houses with insecticides and removing the breeding sites of the larvae. *Culex pipiens* may be found hibernating indoors but does not bother us; there may be present at the same time *Theobaldia annulata* which wakes up at times and attacks man. *Anopheles maculipennis* is a carrier of malaria. Certain characteristic differences between the two kinds of mosquitoes (of which there are many species) are shown in the illustrations (**153, 154**).

Breathing appendages ('tails', pad-like gills, etc.) are as usual absent from larvae which live surrounded by fresh air, such as that of another syrphid (**149**) of the kind which prey on aphids. They breathe in the normal adult way, through spiracles.

Sub-Order *NEMATOCERA*

This sub-order includes the most primitive flies. Besides the Crane-flies or Daddy-long-legs (family Tipulidae, *Tipula maxima,* **144**) whose larvae are especially destructive to roots, there are species which are of great medical importance because of their being disease-transmitting mosquitoes of the family Culicidae. Midge-bites are due to members of the family Ceratopogonidae. In the family Cecidomyiidae, the gall-midges, are many species of economic interest due to their destructive attacks on cereals. Many of the gnats whose larvae feed on fungi are members of the family Mycetophilidae.

Sub-Order *BRACHYCERA*

The females of horse flies and clegs (family Tabanidae) are noisy insects which are blood-suckers of cattle, inflicting painful bites. *Tabanus bromius* (**155**), a gad-fly, is common during the warmer months of the year. Male tabanids visit flowers. The Asilidae, robber-flies, form the largest family of the sub-order. They are hunters of other insects which they catch on the wing. The illustrations of the large *Asilus crabroniformis* (**156**) and the very common *Dioctria rufipes* (**157**) show their characteristic powerful legs. The family Bombyliidae, bee-flies, as instanced by *Bombylius major* (**158**), resemble bumble bees in appearance; the larvae of many species of this family are parasites of bees, such as *Andrena* and *Halictus*.

Sub-Order *CYCLORRHAPHA*

Among the hover flies (family Syrphidae) is another mimic of bumble bees. It is *Volucella bombylans* (**159**), a species which varies much in colouring, and the larvae of which are found in the nests of bees. They have also been found in those of the wasp *Vespula germanica*, to which of course the

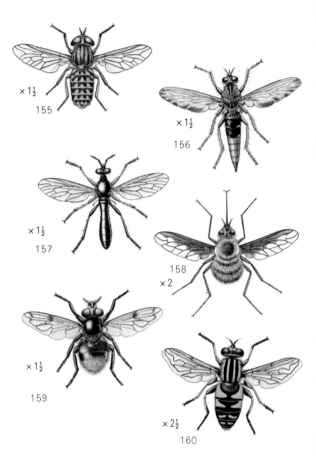

155 Gad-fly, *Tabanus bromius*, **156** Robber-fly, *Asilus crabroniformis*, **157** Robber-fly, *Dioctria rufipes*, **158** Bee-fly, *Bombylius major*, **159** Hover-fly, *Volucella bombylans*, **160** Hover-fly, *Helophilus pendulus*

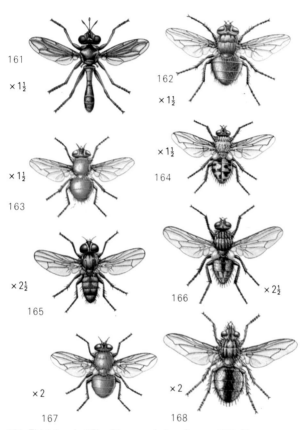

161 Thick-headed Fly, *Physocephala rufipes*,   **162** Blue-bottle, *Calliphora vomitoria*,   **163** Greenbottle, *Lucilia caesar*,   **164** Cluster-fly, *Pollenia rudis*,   **165** Lesser House-fly, *Fannia canicularis*,   **166** Common House-fly, *Musca domestica*,   **167** Greenbottle, *Neomyia cornicina*, **168** Parasitic Fly, *Echinomya fera*

127

imago bears no resemblance. The more familiar colouring of a hover fly is to be seen in the common *Helophilus pendulus* (**160**). Members of the family Conopidae are internal parasites of adult wasps and bees; *Physocephala rufipes* (**161**) resembles a sand wasp (*Ammophila* **220–1**), of the family Sphecidae.

One of the housewife's pet aversions is the Bluebottle, also referred to as the Blow-fly. The Greenbottle is just as unpopular. The insects (all belonging to the family Calliphoridae) enter the kitchen to lay eggs on meat, etc., for their larvae are scavengers. *Calliphora vomitoria* (**162**) is the common Bluebottle. *Lucilia caesar* (**163**) is the common Greenbottle, which seldom enters houses. Numbers of *Pollenia rudis* (**164**), the Cluster-fly, occasionally enter attics. They keep closely together in clusters when at rest indoors, hence their name. Included in the family Muscidae we have the Common House-fly, *Musca domestica* (**166**) a constant companion in man's dwellings. Another is *Fannia canicularis* (**165**) the Lesser House Fly. *Neomyia cornicina* (**167**) is another common Greenbottle.

A true parasite lives entirely at the expense of its host. The family Tachinidae (also called Larvaevoridae) are of this kind, especially prevalent in larvae and pupae of butterflies and moths, they also attack spiders and other arthropods. Parasitic larvae do not attack vital parts of the host, or they would be unable to complete their own development, but when the time for pupation comes they bring about the host's death. The tachinid *Echinomya fera* (**168**) parasitizes larvae of the order

Lepidoptera, including the caterpillar of the Large White Butterfly, *Pieris brassicae* which is a pest of cabbage.

Not all dipterous parasites cause the death of the host, especially when the latter is large, but much distress results from such parasitism. One of the best known of this type of fly is *Gasterophilus intestinalis* (**169**) the common Bot-fly that attacks horses. Its eggs are licked up by the animal in whose stomach the larvae are then able to develop. The fly is now usually included in the extensive family Oestridae, the larvae of which are all internal parasites of large mammals, but it was formerly included in the Muscidae.

There is a group of true flies, the Pupipara, which have become exclusively external parasites of warm-blooded animals and birds. They exhibit remarkable structural changes of a degenerate kind, the result of their highly specialized parasitical habits. Among the family Hippoboscidae there is *Ornithomya avicularia* (**171**) a common blood-sucking parasite of birds. Some species are entirely devoid of wings, such as *Melophagus ovinus* (**170**) which lives in the fleece of sheep. It is known as the Sheep-ked, Sheep-louse or Sheep-tick. The family Nycteribiidae consists of small parasites of bats. Our largest species, *Phthiridium biarticulata* (**172**) is very spider-like in appearance, but it has only the six legs of adult insects. The prominent, well-developed claws of these insects are characteristic of parasites which cling to hosts.

The foregoing species (of the group Pupipara, 'pupa-bearing') lay a fully developed larva, which

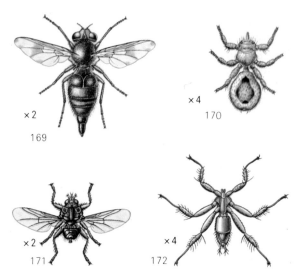

169 Horse Bot-fly, *Gasterophilus intestinalis*,   **170** Sheep-ked, *Melophagus ovinus*,   **171** Bird parasite, *Ornithomya avicularia*,   **172** Bat parasite, *Phthiridium biarticulata*

immediately pupates. The family Braulidae, also wingless parasites, lay eggs, and because of this there are objections to including them with the Pupipara. Braulidae are parasites of bees. *Braula coeca* (**173**) is the Bee-louse, well known to bee-keepers.

FLEAS Order Siphonaptera

Description. Small, flat insects, some without eyes. Antennae short and thick. Mouthparts adapted for piercing and sucking. The adult insects only are parasites of mammals and birds. Metamorphosis complete.

Classification. The order is divided into three distinct families. Also called APHANIPTERA. (57 British species.)

The classification of insects followed in this book illustrates the evolutionary progress of insects, and we see to what degree of perfection evolution has attained in the two orders, the Hymenoptera and Diptera. The comity of insects as arranged by entomologists into scientific groupings is more than a convenience for classification: it permits us, in addition, to appreciate more fully the interrelationship existing between species. It may show, for instance, how a family specialization has changed in one or more related species. To an enquiring mind this gives rise to interesting speculation, which to produce useful conclusions will need to be stimulated by extensive scientific knowledge—such as that of biochemistry, much of which is, however, still shrouded in mystery.

Siphonaptera, fleas, have always been a puzzle to the entomologist. They are not closely related to any other order of insects, and no trace of wings can be found in them. Unlike primitive insects, they undergo complete metamorphosis—even a cocoon is present. It is therefore most likely that fleas early

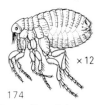

173 Bee-louse, *Braula coeca, irritans*

174 Human Flea, *Pulex*

in their evolutionary history became specialized parasites. We have seen how in the order Diptera (flies) certain species (Pupipara) have degenerated in structure through having become specialized parasites. In some respects the present order, the members of which are exclusively parasitic, shows a very distant relationship to flies.

Fleas live by sucking the blood of mammals and birds, many of them being confined to a particular species. They shun light and are attracted to body-warmth. The fleas on a dead animal will forsake it on the approach of a warm-blooded creature, which has not necessarily to be its normal host. The fleas of a rat which has died from plague may leap on to a passing man, thus providing the essential conditions for transmitting the dreaded disease. The bacillus of bubonic plague is introduced by a complicated method of inoculation (i.e. by scratching bacillus-infected flea excreta beneath the skin).

Only the adult flea is a blood-sucker. When eggs are produced they fall off the host on to the ground or floor of the places it frequents. On emergence the larva, which has no eyes or legs, feeds on detritus; it is not a parasite, so the larvae of the Human Flea, *Pulex irritans* (**174**), is consequently found only in dwellings of unclean people. After undergoing two moults, the larva spins a cocoon, in which it remains for a variable time until stimulated by external vibrations, such as may happen when a person enters a room. Emergence then occurs, and is consequently at a most suitable moment for leaping on to a host.

SAWFLIES, ANTS, BEES, WASPS,
ICHNEUMONS, GALL WASPS
Order Hymenoptera

Description. Four membranous wings, the hind smaller than the fore wings and having interlocking hooklets allowing fore and hind wings to act as one. Mouthparts adapted for biting, lapping or sucking. Ovipositor always present but may be functionally modified for sawing or stinging. Metamorphosis complete.

Classification. Two sub-orders, *SYMPHYTA*, having no marked constriction or waist between the abdomen and thorax, and thus also referred to as *SESSILIVENTRES*—trochanters 2-jointed, larvae generally possessing thoracic and abdominal legs; and *APOCRITA* with the waist generally very evident, hence also referred to as *PETIOLATA*—trochanters 1- or 2-jointed, larvae legless.

The Apocrita are for convenience divided into *ACULEATA*, the stinging forms, and the *PARASITICA*, which parasitize other insects. There are over 6,600 British species.

Hymenoptera is the order to which the least justice can be done in any popular book on insects. This is due not only to the exceedingly vast number of species, but especially also to their highly evolved life-histories. The different species have habits that are most complex, and at the same time differ very much from each other. Thus any descriptions chosen can only illustrate isolated examples of the wonders to be observed in other species.

All hymenopterous species undergo the complete cycle of insect metamorphosis, egg, larva, pupa and imago all being present. An important feature is that the majority of their larvae must be provided by the parents with food, as they are unable to seek it themselves. Thus in what are known as the 'solitary' species, the female has to make all arrangements for concealing her egg (or eggs) and providing food adjacent to it for the larva when it emerges. Some of these solitary species live in colonies, but each individual works independently for its progeny. Evolution has progressed further in what are known as the 'social' species, as instanced by ants and many bees and wasps, whose division of labour for the provision of food for future generations becomes highly complex. The advanced degree of social behaviour attained in Hymenoptera is equalled only by one other order, the Isoptera (termites), but these insects do not occur in the British Isles.

An anatomical feature of great importance in connection with the behaviour of many of these insects is the ovipositor (egg-placer). It is used for penetrating matter in which the female wishes to lay

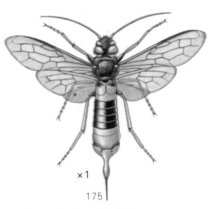

×1

175

175 Greater Horntail. *Uroceras gigas*

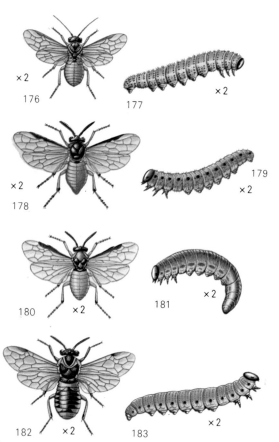

Sawflies with their larvae: **176** Gooseberry Sawfly, *Nematus ribesii*, **177** its larva, **178** Poplar Sawfly, *Trichiocampus viminalis*, **179** its larva, **180** Turnip Sawfly, *Athalia rosae*, **181** its larva, **182** Pine Sawfly, *Diprion pini*, **183** its larva her eggs. In some species the ovipositor is modified for sawing, boring, piercing or stinging. The stinging apparatus consists of two poison glands (page 17), these being highly specialized.

Sub-Order Symphyta. *Sawflies, and Horntails or Woodwasps*

This sub-order is sometimes called PHYTOPHAGA, plant-eaters, or SESSILIVENTRES because the abdomen is broadly sessile with the thorax (i.e., there is no constriction between these two parts of the body). Its members are less specialized than those of the second sub-order (APOCRITA), but the ovipositor is modified for sawing or boring. The larvae also differ in that they fend for themselves, being provided with true (thoracic) legs as well as six or more pairs of abdominal prolegs, the latter of course being present only during larval life as in the case of caterpillars of butterflies and moths (LEPIDOPTERA).

The SYMPHYTA are divided into six super-families. One of these, the ORUSSOIDEA, may be mentioned here because there is only one rare British species. Parasitism, general as it is in hymenopterous insects, is known in SYMPHYTA only in the one species of the genus *Orussus* in which the larva is a parasite of timber beetles.

The interesting Siricidae, known as horntails or woodwasps, is a family of large brilliantly coloured insects whose larvae are wood-borers of trees. The Greater Horntail, *Urocerus gigas*, (**175**) of fir woods, is the largest species we have. It is typical of its kind in appearance and colouring, though several species are metallic-blue. It is often mistaken for the Hornet (**202**) because of its sting-like projection, which is the ovipositor of the female, and the black-and-yellow arrangement of its col-

184 Sawfly larva on leaf, showing characteristic attitude ×3

ours. The ovipositor of the Horntail is used for boring into bark to deposit an egg in the wood. The larva bores into the heart of the tree, and can do considerable damage; there are several records of Horntails emerging from wood that was covered by sheet metal.

In sawflies, the ovipositor is modified into a saw, enabling these insects literally to saw leaves and make incisions in plant stems. *Abia sericea* is an example of the leaf-eating sawflies. The stem sawflies (Cephidae) are a family of small insects whose larvae bore in the stems and shoots of plants to feed upon the pith. The larger sawflies belong to other families, the majority to Tenthredinidae.

Leaf-eating larvae bear much resemblance to the caterpillars of butterflies and moths. They may be distinguished from them in that the Sawfly larvae have (in addition to three pairs of thoracic legs) six or more pairs of abdominal legs (prolegs), whereas in butterflies and moths there are never more than five pairs. When fully grown the larvae make cocoons on the food-plants or, less frequently, in the soil. Sawflies are best known in their larval state, and this is especially so in those found on roses and fruit-bushes. Like caterpillars, they are of various colours, and they have a peculiar habit of curling the posterior segments of the body away from the leaf on which they are feeding (**184**). The following larvae are well known.

Nematus ribesii (**177**), larva of the Gooseberry Sawfly (**176**, female). Also found on currants.

Trichiocampus viminalis (**179**), larva of the Poplar Sawfly (**178**).

Athalia rosae (**181**), larva of the Turnip Sawfly (**180**, female).

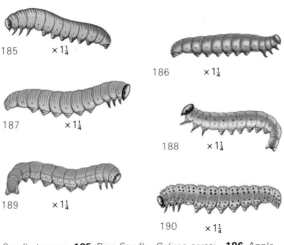

Sawfly larvae: **185** Pine Sawfly. *Caliroa cerasi*. **186** Apple Sawfly. *Hoplocampa testudinea* **187** *Allantus cinctus*. **188** *Blennocampa pusilla*. **189** Palisade Sawfly. *Stauronematus compressicornis*. **190** *Arge ochropus*

Diprion pini (**183**), larva of the Pine Sawfly (**182**, female).

Caliroa cerasi (**185**) feeds on oak, birch and willow, being one of the larvae popularly referred to as slugworms, which are also found on roses.

Hoplocampa testudinea (**186**) larva of the Apple Sawfly; it feeds on the newly-formed fruit.

Allantus cinctus (**187**) is a rose-leaf feeder.

Blennocampa pusilla (**188**) also feeds on rose leaves, concealing itself whilst doing so by turning the edge of the leaf over itself.

Stauronematus compressicornis (**189**) feeds on poplar, and is the famous Palisade Sawfly larva, so-called because it forms with saliva a series of little posts round the area of the leaf on which it is feeding.

Arge ochropus (= *rosae*) (**190**). Common on roses, southern half of England.

Sub-Order Apocrita. *Ants, Bees, Wasps, Ichneumons, Gall Wasps*

All members of this sub-order have a well-defined (petiolate) waist, hence these insects are also called Petiolata. They have also been called Heterophaga, suggesting their varied diet. There are numerous species of Apocrita, all having extremely varied and interesting life-histories. The adults are usually highly specialized in their habits, which in some species has resulted in the forming of social communities. Most Hymenoptera belong to the present sub-order which may be divided further into *PARASITICA*, comprising insects of specialized parasitical habits, and *ACULEATA*, species having stings.

APOCRITA

Super-families	Families	Popular names
PARASITICA (Parasitical species)		
ICHNEUMONOIDEA	Ichneumonidae	Ichneumon-wasps
	Braconidae	Ichneumon-wasps
CHALCIDOIDEA	Chalcididae	Chalcids
CYNIPOIDEA	Cynipidae	Gall Wasps
ACULEATA (Stinging species)		
FORMICOIDEA	Formicidae	Ants
VESPOIDEA	Vespidae	Wasps
	Eumenidae	Solitary Wasps, Potter and Mason Wasps
POMPILOIDEA	Pompilidae	Spider Wasps
SPHECOIDEA	Sphecidae	Digger Wasps
APOIDEA	Andrenidae	Mining Bees
	Megachilidae	Leaf-cutter Bees
	Nomadidae	Homeless Bees
	Anthrophoridae	Potter Bees
	Bombidae	Bumble or Humble Bees
	Apidae	Hive Bees

The literature on the Parasitica and Aculeata is vast and the amount added to it every year reflects the importance of many of these insects' activities to man's economy. Many Parasitica, for example, have furnished allies to combat pestiferous insects; nearly all of the latter belong to other orders.

The diversity of habits may be gathered from the popular names given to some of these insect families, as given opposite:

PARASITICA. The most important parasites which limit the unchecked multiplication of the insect legions belong to the extensive super-families of Ichneumonoidea (ichneumon-wasps) and Chalcidoidea (chalcids). The latter are less known, but they are of even greater importance than the ichneumons.

Ichneumons are slender insects with long antennae, which are constantly in motion. The antennae—and, of course, the four wings of all members of the order Hymenoptera—readily distinguish them from true flies (order Diptera). The appearance of our largest species, *Rhyssa persuasoria* (**191**) is typical of an ichneumon, the long ovipositor showing that this one is a female. In some mysterious way this insect is able to detect where the larva of the Greater Horntail (**175** shows the female imago) lies concealed within the tree. It then proceeds to bore into the wood with its flimsy-looking ovipositor in order to lay an egg on or near the larva. On emergence the ichneumon larva will feed on that of the sawfly, which it will destroy. The Horntail and its parasite are confined to pinewoods, and are therefore not seen as frequently as the

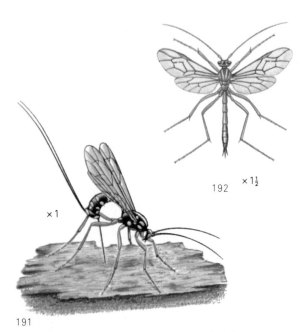

×1

192 ×1½

191

Ichneumons: **191** *Rhyssa persuasoria*, **192** Common Yellow Ophion, *Ophion luteus*

Common Yellow Ophion, *Ophion luteus* (**192**), an ichneumon which parasitizes caterpillars of several of our larger moths, such as that of the Puss Moth. Illustration **193** shows the claw it uses to hold the victim while the egg is laid.

Parasitism of every conceivable form exists, and insects in all stages of development are subject to attack. The relationship between species of the group Parasitica and their hosts is often very specifically restricted (e.g., between *Rhyssa persuasoria* and the Greater Horntail), and this has permitted many spectacular successes of applied entomology to be achieved under the heading of biological control. An incident of this type of parasitism is shown (**194-5**).

Gall wasps belong to the family Cynipidae and are parasites of plants and trees. Some of these small insects are gall-causers on leaves, flowers, stems and roots; others do not cause galls, but live as lodgers, taking up residence with a gall-causer, with whom they then live in close proximity without doing any harm to the rightful owner. These lodgers may be other cynipids, or larvae of butterflies or moths, beetles or true flies. There are yet other species which are true parasites of other Cynipidae.

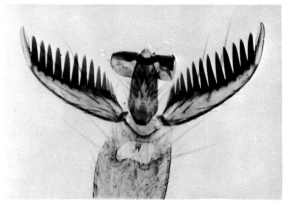

193 Claw of an Ichneumon × 60

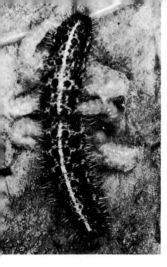

194 *(left)* Larvae of an ichneumon, family Braconidae, crawling out of caterpillar of Large White Butterfly. × 1½
195 *(right)* Two minutes later there is no trace of the larvae, as they have immediately spun their cocoons. The host caterpillar now dies and will shrivel up × 1½

The galls are caused by the living larva (**196–7**) after emergence from the egg, the presence of which modifies the form taken by the growing plant tissues. A remarkable feature of galls is that the form and colour of a gall on a particular plant or tree will be characteristic of a definite species of insect. Galls are in fact as varied as the insects themselves. It appears, however, that insects of the same genus produce galls of a similar type even on plants that are not closely related. Not all galls are due to insects, however.

ACULEATA. The ovipositor of these insects is

modified into a sting, and can no longer be used for laying eggs. The eggs are laid from an opening at the base of the ovipositor. In ants the sting is present only in the females and workers in the case of a number of carnivorous species. In other ants the sting is vestigial or absent, and these species are considered to be more evolved; furthermore, they have become vegetarian—as are most British species.

All ants belong to the family Formicidae. Ants pair in a nuptial or marriage flight; the female on descending to earth rids herself of her wings and seeks a suitable site wherein to prepare a brood chamber. She will never leave this chamber, where she lays her first eggs. When the larvae appear they are fed with secretions from her salivary glands. After a while the larvae pupate, and eventually adult ants emerge. These are workers who henceforth relieve their mother of all cares. They make a

196 *(left)* Pupa of Oak Apple Gall Wasp, *Biorhiza pallida* × 2
197 *(right)* Pupa of Marble Gall Wasp, *Andricus kollari* × 4

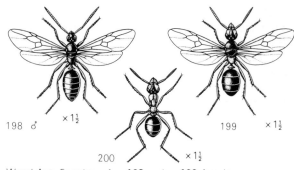

198 ♂ ×1½

200 ×1½

199 ×1½

Wood Ant, *Formica rufa*: **198** male, **199** female, **200** worker

passage from the brood chamber to the outside world, where they forage for food. The mother or queen now attends to nothing else but egg-laying; she is fed by the workers. Some females have been known to live like this for fifteen years. In midsummer, males and females appear which at a chosen moment fly away on their marriage flight. One of our most familiar species is the Wood Ant, *Formica rufa* (**198**—male, **199**—female, both shown with wings 'set', **200**—worker, which never has wings). Ants form permanent communities of numerous individuals. The Wood Ant nest, for example, may have a population of as many as 100,000 individuals; in another species 500,000 ants were found in one formicary. During 1977 ecologists of the University of Lausanne discovered the largest known colony of red ants. They estimated that some 300 million were living in 1,200 'hills' linked by 60 miles of 'paths' spread over 170 acres of forest in the Jura mountains.

Other social insects are the wasps (family Vespidae), such as *Vespula vulgaris*, the Common Wasp (queen—**201**) our only Hornet, *Vespa crabro* (queen—**202**) as well as the bumble bees (family Apidae) whose workers are well known, such as *Bombus lapidarius* (**207**), *B. pratorum* (**208**), *B. terrestris* (**209**). *Apis mellifera* (queen—**210**,

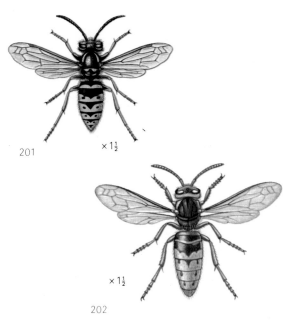

201 × 1½

× 1½

202

Queens: **201** Common Wasp, *Vespula vulgaris*, **202** Hornet, *Vespa crabro*

147

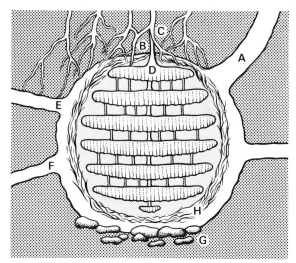

203 Underground nest of wasp, *Vespula germanica* × 1

A—entrance   E, F—side galleries
B—attachment to root   G—detritus at bottom
C—root   H—surrounding envelope
D—first comb

drone—**211**, worker—**212**) is the common Hive
Bee. There is considerable variation in the habits
and life-histories of different species of social
insects. The underground nest of a common social
insect, the wasp *Vespula germanica*, is shown (**203**).

Social species have close relatives who are parasites on them. *Psithyrus campestris* (**213**—female) is
a Cuckoo Bee parasite of *Bombus*; after killing the
Bombus queen she lays her own eggs, the *Psithyrus*
larvae being cared for by the *Bombus* workers. Of
the velvet ants (family Mutillidae, which are not

204 ×1¼   205 ×1¼

Velvet Ant, *Mutilla europaea:* **204** male, **205** female

ants, however) *Multilla europaea* (male—**204**, female—**205**, also parasitizes *Bombus*. The males are winged, the females wingless, in all species. The larvae of *Chrysis ignita* (**214**) one of the ruby-tails (family Chrysididae), feed upon other members of the order Hymenoptera.

Other species lead blameless lives. *Eumenes coarctatus* (**215**) is a potter wasp of the family Eumenidae, named after its small pot-shaped nest. Spider wasps (Pompilidae, an extensive family) paralyze spiders by stinging them; they do not kill

206 Gooden's Homeless Bee, *Nomada goodeniana* × 5

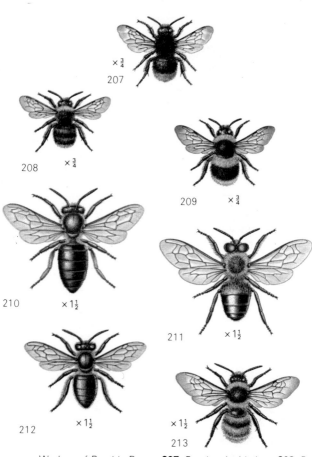

Workers of Bumble Bees: **207** *Bombus lapidarius*, **208** *B Pratorum*, **209** *B. terrestris*; Hive Bee, *Apis mellifera*: **210** queen, **211** drone, **212** worker; **213** Cuckoo Bee, *Psithyrus campestris*

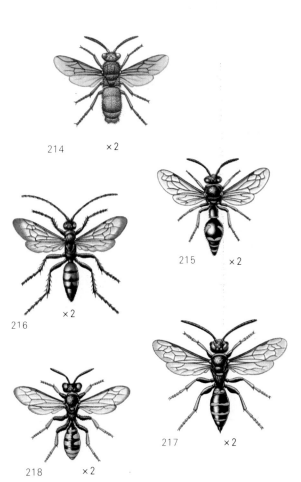

214 Ruby-tail, *Chrysis ignita*. 215 Potter Wasp, *Eumenes coarctatus*. 216 Spider Wasp, *Anoplius viaticus*. 217 *Crabro cribarius*. 218 *Gorytes mystaccus*

151

219 The cells of leaf-cutter bees, Megachilidae, are made from circles cut out from rose leaves, petals etc. × 4

them. *Anoplius viaticus* (**216**) buries such victims in an excavated hole, an egg being laid on each spider so that the larva on emergence will have a provision of preserved food. Such insects are solitary species, as are members of Sphecidae wasps (**217–8**, **220–21** being examples) and of *Prosopis* bees (**222**). Another genus, *Andrena* (*A. armata* **223**) also comprises solitary species, though the females of these tend to congregate in colonies. They are parasitized by species of the genus *Nomada*, such as Gooden's Homeless Bee, *Nomada goodeniana* (**206**) and *Nomada marshamella* (**224**—male). *Megachile maritima* (**225**—male) belongs to the family Megachilidae, leaf-cutters, whose work is illustrated (**219**). The family also includes parasitic and other species.

BEETLES Order Coleoptera

Description. Minute to large insects, usually with hard bodies. The fore wings modified into horny elytra (wing-cases), hind wings membranous and folded below the elytra, or absent. Biting mouthparts. Tarsi 5-jointed. Metamorphosis complete.

Classification. Two sub-orders. The *ADEPHAGA*, have usually threadlike antennae. Both larvae and adults (imagines) are carnivorous. The *POLYPHAGA* have very varied antennae and tarsi. Feeding habits vary greatly. (Over 4,000 British species.)

Beetles are numerous everywhere, yet they are seldom seen. This is because they lead an unobtrusive life, being concealed from view, or nocturnal. Even the imagines are seldom seen by the admittedly notoriously unobservant non-naturalist, though we ourselves have nevertheless to search for them if we wish to see specimens. Everyone, however, knows the ladybird beetle, and perhaps the tiger beetle. These two exemplify the general aspect of beetles as a whole. Although the order is exceedingly vast—over a quarter of a million species are already known to science—its members are somehow readily classed as beetles by the non-expert, but the family Staphylinidae (page 160) are perhaps rather puzzling when seen for the first time.

Beetles are essentially creatures of the soil itself. There they hunt other insects or beetles. They live in refuse of all kinds, vegetable or animal, and in decaying organic matter. Many live in sound or in rotting wood, and yet other species feed on plants and trees and the fruits they bear. Every form of animal and vegetable product, dried or processed by man, has one or more coleopterous species that will feed upon it. Beetles of the genus *Anthrenus* attack the carefully dried treasures of museums, and they breed there, too, so that after a time many exhibits could be destroyed. Some beetles even live

153

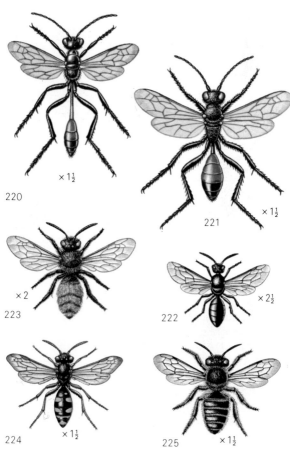

220 Sand Wasp, *Ammophila sabulosa*. **221** *A. hirsuta*.
222 *Prosopis signata*. **223** *Andrena armata*. **224** *Nomada marshamella*. **225** Leaf-cutter Bee, *Megachile maritima*

154

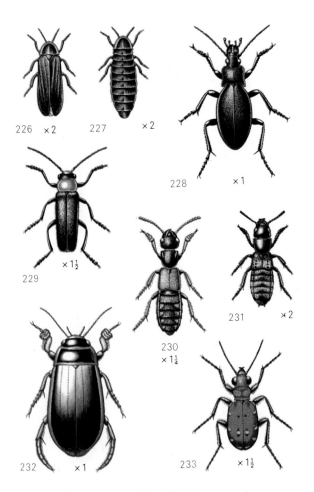

226 *Lampyris noctiluca*, male. **227** Glow-worm, *L. noctiluca*, female. **228** *Carabus violaceus*. **229** *Cantharis abdominalis*. **230** Rove Beetle, *Staphylinus caesareus*. **231** *Creophilus maxillosus*. **232** Great Diving Beetle, *Dytiscus marginalis*. **233** Tiger Beetle, *Cicindela campestris*

by the sea and are regularly submerged by the tides.

The diversity of the food environment where the beetle larvae develop means that every form of adaptation is to be met with. Essentially the range of anatomical difference between larvae is due to the manner in which the food has to be obtained. If it is done by hunting, then the larva is active on its legs and has properly developed jaws for seizing prey. The larva of the ladybird is of this type (**259**); so is that of ground beetles (**234**) and of the Great Diving Beetle, which lives in ponds (**12**). When a larva develops surrounded by its food, such as the wood-feeders, then the jaws are adapted for their purpose and the legs are weak; in others the legs may be wanting and eyes may be entirely absent as well. The carabid larva referred to above (**234**) on the other hand, may have six simple eyes (*ocelli*), of great value to a hunter. When the larvae are full-grown they turn into pupae, usually with no protective covering, as in butterflies and moths, because the surroundings where pupation takes

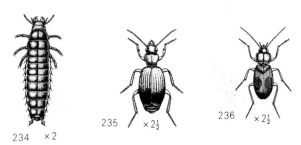

235   ×2½

236   ×2½

234   ×2

234 Carabid larva.   **235** Bombardier Beetle, *Brachinus crepitans*.   **236** *Badister bipustulatus*

place afford all the safety needed. The time taken for larval development varies greatly, depending on the nutritional value of the food. Wood-feeders may take two or three years before reaching full growth.

Sub-Order Adephaga. *Carnivorous Beetles*

This sub-order is noted for its predaceous carnivorous species, both terrestrial (*Carabidae*, Tiger and Ground Beetles) and aquatic (*Dytiscidae*, Water Beetles and *Gyrinidae*, Whirligigs). The *Carabidae* comprise two sub-families, the *Cicindelinae* and *Carabinae*, which were once classed as distinct families.

The larvae of the sub-order Adephaga are as predaceous as the adult insects. That of *Cicindela campestris*, the well-known Tiger Beetle, is, however, rather sluggish. It waits hidden in a vertical position in a hole in the ground, only the jaws projecting above the surface, and with these it seizes any small living prey that passes: the victims are devoured at the bottom of the hole. This beetle (**233**) frequents sandy places in spring and early summer. *C. sylvatica* is a close relation of more sombre colour. Among the sub-family Carabinae the common *Carabus nemoralis* and *C. violaceus* (**228**) belong to the species described by Fabre as frenzied murderers. Carabid larvae (**234**) are just as fierce. Not quite so closely related is the Bombardier Beetle, *Brachinus crepitans* (**235**), so named because if chased it can squirt out with an explosive noise a liquid which volatizes immediately on reaching the air; this method of defence is present in several species. *Badister bipustulatus* (**236**) is common in

×¾

237 Great
Silver Water
Beetle. *Hydro-
philus piceus*

marshy places; it is slightly smaller than a similar
species, *B. unipustulatus*, from which it differs
particularly in the shape of the thorax.

The aquatic members of the sub-order Adephaga
are as fierce as the terrestrial forms. The Great
Diving Beetle, *Dytiscus marginalis* (**232**) if kept in
an aquarium, will soon destroy every living creature
in it. The male has on the front legs remarkable
disc-like suckers used for grasping the female.
Unlike most aquatic larvae, that of *Dytiscus* cannot
breathe in water, and so it has to go to the surface as
the imagines are obliged to do. Air is taken in by
protruding the hind quarters out of the water. Quite
the opposite obtains in the largest of all water
beetles, *Hydrophilus piceus* (**237**), the adult of which
protrudes its head-end out of the water to obtain air.
This is the Great Silver Water Beetle, named after
the bubble of air which covers its underside as it
swims down. The imago of this beetle is vegetarian.
It does not belong to the sub-order Adephaga, but
is of the family Hydrophilidae of the sub-order
Polyphaga. Its larva is, however, carnivorous.

Sub-Order Polyphaga. *Omnivorous Beetles*

The members of this sub-order are most diverse in anatomy and biology. They are also exceedingly numerous, the species being classified into families, super-families and larger groupings. A clear and useful idea of them can be obtained by setting out a simplified list as given below, and this also indicates the scientific families corresponding to popular names of the more common beetles, some of which are referred to in this book. The Polyphaga comprise eighteen super-families with well over one hundred families.

POLYPHAGA*

Super-families	Families	Popular Names
HYDROPHILOIDEA	Hydrophilidae	Land and Water Scavenger Beetles
STAPHYLINOIDEA	Silphidae	Burying and Carrion Beetles
	Staphylinidae	Rove Beetles
SCARABAEOIDEA	Lucanidae	Stag Beetles
	Scarabaeidae	Chafers, Dung Beetles
ELATEROIDEA	Elateridae	Click Beetles
CANTHAROIDEA	Lampyridae	Glow-worms
	Cantharidae	Soldier Beetles
BOSTRYCHOIDEA	Anobiidae	Wood-borer Beetles
	Lyctidae	Powder Post Beetles
CUCUJOIDEA	Coccinellidae	Ladybird Beetles
	Tenebrionidae	Nocturnal Ground Beetles
	Pyrochroidae	Cardinal Beetles
	Meloidae	Oil Beetles, Blister Beetles
CHRYSOMELOIDEA	Cerambycidae	Longhorn Beetles
	Chrysomelidae	Leaf Beetles
CURCULIONOIDEA	Curculionidae	Weevils, Bark Beetles

* *This list does not give a complete picture of our 'omnivorous' species, but is comprehensive in respect of our commoner Polyphaga.*

238 Rove Beetle, *Staphylinus caesareus*, **239** Devil's Coach-horse, *Staphylinus olens*

We can allow ourselves here only a few general remarks on the Polyphaga of which some family representatives are illustrated.

An important anatomical feature characteristic of beetles is the pair of hard wing-cases, or elytra. In some species the elytra are, however, much reduced in length, exposing to view the abdominal segments. This is to be seen in the numerous rove beetles (family Staphylinidae), such as *Staphylinus caesareus* (**230, 238**), where the reduced elytra are well shown. This allows much flexibility of the abdomen. *Staphylinus olens*, the Devil's Coach-horse (**239**), makes use of this to oppose danger by adopting a threatening attitude and emitting at the same time an unpleasant smell. The common *Creophilus maxillosus* (**231**) is another example from this family. The most interesting oil beetles (family Meloidae) have similarly abbreviated elytra, as in *Meloe proscarabaeus* (**240–1**). The well known Glow-worm is the female of *Lampyris noctiluca* (family Lampyridae) in which all the abdominal segments are exposed (**227**); the male (**226**) has, however, complete elytra, as well as wings to take him to the female's 'cold light', which is a sexual call.

×1¼ 240 ♂ 241 ×1¼

Oil Beetle, *Meloe proscarabaeus:* **240** male, **241** female

Cantharis abdominalis (**229**) is a representative
of the family Cantharidae, whose members have no
photogenic (light-producing) organs as possessed
by their cousins the Lampyridae. Other species,
forming also part of the superfamily Diversicornia,
are *Ampedus balteatus* often found in large numbers
on birch, though it is not common everywhere;
Cantharis rustica (**244**), which is common on
flowers and shrubs; *Agriotes obscurus* is unfor-
tunately all too common, its larvae being probably
the commonest of our 'wireworms'. *Necrobia ruficollis* (**242**) is another member; it is found in dry
carcases and skins, and among bones. The species is
celebrated among coleopterists because, in the
words of Canon Fowler, it "saved the life of the
celebrated Latreille: when imprisoned at Bordeaux
during the French Revolution, he found a specimen
of the insect on the walls of his cell, and sent it to M.
Bory de St. Vincent, whom he knew to be interested
in entomology, and who had influence enough to
secure his release".

161

242 ×4

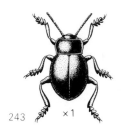

243 ×1

242 *Necrobia ruficollis,* **243** Bloody-nosed Beetle, *Timarcha tenebricosa*

The super-family Heteromera is named after the uneven number of joints in the tarsi of the insects comprising it, there being only four joints in the hind legs, while the two other pairs have five joints. Included in it is *Pyrochroa coccinea* (**245**), of the small family Pyrochroidae, the Cardinal Beetles, which may be found under the bark of decaying oak. The black head of the species distinguishes it immediately from *Pyrochroa serraticornis,* whose head is red; this beetle is also smaller, and it is found on flowers and grasses.

Meloe proscarabaeus may be mentioned further as an example of 'reflex-bleeding' (see page 17); another is *Timarcha tenebricosa* (**243**), popularly called the Bloody-nosed Beetle because it pours out a red fluid ('blood') from its mouth when it is touched or alarmed. The latter species, and *Chrysolina staphylaea* (**246**), belong to the Chrysomelidae, a most extensive family of leaf-eaters. Another member is the redoubtable *Leptinotarsa decemlineata* (**247**), the Colorado Beetle, which came from America in 1875 and

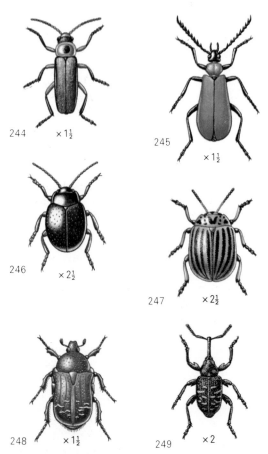

244 *Cantharis rustica.* **245** Cardinal Beetle, *Pyrochroa coccinea.* **246** *Chrysolina staphylaea.* **247** Colorado Beetle, *Leptinotarsa decemlineata.* **248** Rose Chafer, *Cetonia aurata.* **249** Weevil, *Hylobius abietis*

successfully established itself across the Channel. The beetle is very destructive to growing potatoes. It has invaded England on several occasions, but so far it has been eliminated, thanks to immediate steps taken by the authorities; when the beetle is discovered it should be reported without delay to the police.

Rhagium bifasciatum (**250**) is found in fir woods. Many beetles of other families are to be found on leaves, though their larvae may feed on roots, etc. One of the most beautiful is *Cetonia aurata* (**248**),

×2

250 *Rhagium bifasciatum*

×2

251 Cockchafer, *Melolontha melolontha*

252 Stag Beetle. *Lucanus cervus* × 1

the common Rose Chafer, as well as the familiar Cockchafer, *Melolontha melolontha* (or *vulgaris*) (**251**), which is particularly 'hairy' when freshly emerged. These two species, included in the family Scarabaeidae, as well as members of the Curculionidae, the weevils, such as *Hylobius abietis* (**249**), are perhaps the best known to non-naturalists. Another familiar beetle, but restricted to southern England, is *Lucanus cervus* (**252**), the Stag Beetle; only the male has the enlarged mandibles, which look like miniature stag antlers. This species varies much in size, and in size and shape of the 'antlers'.

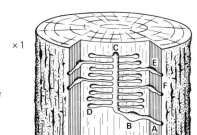

×1

A—entrance
B—nuptial chamber
C—central gallery
D—larval galleries
E—pupal chamber
F—exit

253 Tunnels made beneath bark by Scolytidae Beetles. Eggs are laid in the central gallery

Other beetles are destructive wood-borers, or live in decaying wood, as do the larvae of the Stag Beetle (**264**). Most of these insects belong to the family Cerambycidae, the Longhorns. They are attractively coloured, as for example the Musk Beetle *Aromia moschata*, (**254**), *Saperda carcharias*, *Strangalia maculata* (**255**) and the active Wasp Beetle, *Clytus arietis* (**256, 265**), which mimics a wasp, particularly deceiving when visiting flowers in sunshine.

Members of the family Scolytidae are bark beetles, though plants and fruits are also attacked by some species. These insects make the intricate tunnels often seen under the bark of many trees (**253**); their life-histories are most interesting.

Some beetles destroy or befoul man's stored food: such are *Tenebrio molitor* (**261**), of the family Tenebrionidae, whose larvae are known to bakers as Mealworms (**262**), and another is *Blaps mucronata* (**263**), which has a particularly unpleasant smell. Its larvae eat decaying vegetable matter in cellars, bakeries and other dark retreats.

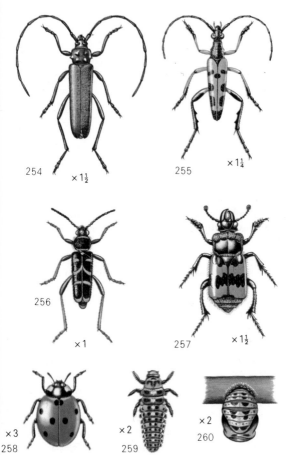

254 Musk Beetle, *Aromia moschata,*   **255** *Strangalia
maculata,*   **256** Wasp Beetle, *Clytus arietis,*
257 *Nicrophorus vespillo,*   **258** Seven-spot Ladybird,
Coccinella septempunctata,   **259** its larva,   **260** its pupa

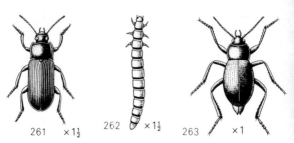

261 *Tenebrio molitor*, **262** Mealworm, larva of *T. molitor*,
263 *Blaps mucronata*

A number of species among the sub-order
Polyphaga are carnivorous, the best-known being
the ladybird beetles (family Coccinellidae), of
which there are several species. They often vary
much in markings, except *Coccinella septempunctata* (**258**, pupa and larva—**259, 260**), the Seven-
spot Ladybird. Both the larvae and the adults feed
voraciously on small insects, especially aphids.
Anatis ocellata, the Eyed Ladybird, is our largest
species; it is found on firs.

Some beetles, such as the family Silphidae, are
useful scavengers of dead animals and birds, both
they and their larvae feeding on them. *Nicrophorus
investigator*, *N. humator*, and *N. vespillo* (**257**) are
examples of beetles which actually bury, say a bird,
by digging the ground away from underneath it,
and there the female will lay her eggs, usually in
pairs. Besides these useful species, known as bury-
ing beetles, there are many carrion beetles which do
not act as sextons, but whose larvae and imagines
help in clearing away carcases. *Oiceoptoma thoracicum* (**266**) will often be found near carrion, to

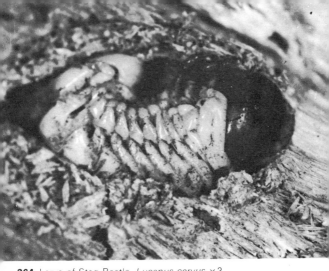

264 Larva of Stag Beetle, *Lucanus cervus* × 3

265 Wasp Beetle, *Clytus arietis* × 2

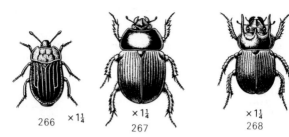

266 *Oiceoptoma thoracicum,*   **267** *Geotrupes stercorarius,*
268 *Typhaeus typhoeus,* male

which it is attracted by the smell of decay, as are all
these beetles. Other beetles with unpleasant but
useful feeding habits belong to the Scarabaeidae, a
family celebrated by Fabre. In addition to the root
and decaying leaf eaters of this family, already
mentioned, there are those who feed on dung
(usually that of herbivorous animals). *Geotrupes
stercorarius* (**267**) sometimes called the Dor Beetle,
is one of these and so is *Typhaeus typhoeus* (**268**—
male; the two thorn-like processes at the front of
the thorax are absent in the female).

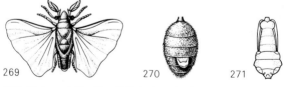

269 *Stylops dalii* × 12,   **270** its larva in the abdomen of a
Bee (enlarged),   **271** its pupa × 8

Description. Minute insects, usually parasites of other insects. Males winged. Branched antennae. Mouthparts degenerate, originally biting type. Fore wings reduced to halteres or balancers, hind wings large. Females degenerate, wingless, usually legless, and have the appearance of larvae.

Classification. There are four British families. The order is closely related to COLEOPTERA, the Beetles. (16 British species.)

The larval stages are passed as internal parasites of certain wasps, such as those of the genera *Vespa*, *Vespula*, and bees, especially *Halictus* and *Andrena*. The female stylops passes the whole of her life in the host, from whose sides the parasite may be seen protruding between the bee's segments. The stylops, or stylopids, absorb body-fluids of the host without destroying the vital organs, but the genitalia are adversely affected. 'Stylopized' hosts may often be recognized by their misshapen abdomen. The males are completely formed insects, having very elaborate antennae. Pairing takes place on the host!

As the eggs develop the female becomes almost completely filled with eggs. The larvae hatch inside the parent from which they later escape. They are very active at this stage of their lives. The bee transports them to its nest where the parasites promptly enter the bee larvae.

CLASS ARACHNIDA

Classification. The order ARANEAE, or spiders, belongs to the class ARACHNIDA, in which are included such varied arthropods (phylum *ARTHROPODA*, or jointed-footed animals) as harvestmen (*OPILIONES*, or *PHALANGIDAE*), false-scorpions (*CHELONETHI*, or *PSEUDO-SCORPIONES*), and mites (*ACARI*), in addition to orders not represented in the British Isles, bringing the total of orders in this class to eleven, one of which is represented only by fossil forms. Different species of Arachnids often bear little resemblance to each other. A spider and the large foreign fish-like king-crab (*Limulus*)—a living fossil with a direct ancestry of millions of years—have no apparent morphological affinity, and indeed this class serves more than anything else as a convenient way of grouping a strange assortment of creatures. There are about 623 British species of spiders.

Description. The differences we notice immediately between spiders and insects are the following:

Spiders	Insects
(*a*) Two divisions of the body, the *cephalo-thorax*, the head-chest—the head and thorax being fused together—and the *abdomen*.	(*a*) Three divisions of the body, *head, thorax* and *abdomen*.
(*b*) Four pairs of legs.	(*b*) Three pairs of legs in adults.
(*c*) No antennae.	(*c*) Almost always with antennae.
(*d*) No wings.	(*d*) Wings usually present.
(*e*) Usually four to eight simple eyes, never compound.	(*e*) Imagines (adult insects) often have two kinds of eyes, compound (multiple-faceted) and simple (ocelli).

172

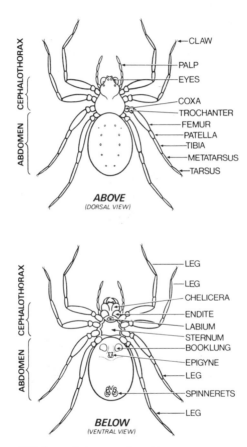

272 External structure of a spider

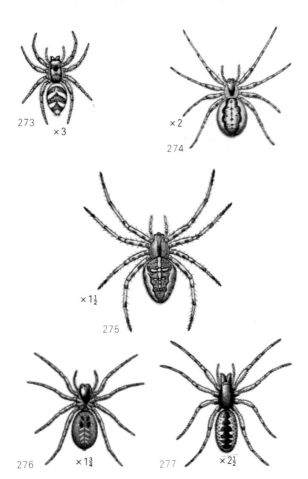

273 ×3

×2
274

×1½

275

276 ×1¾

277 ×2½

Female spiders: **273** Zebra Spider, *Salticus scenicus*.
274 *Zygiella x-notata*. **275** Garden Spider, *Araneus diadematus*. **276** *Amaurobius similis*. **277** *Segestria senoculata*

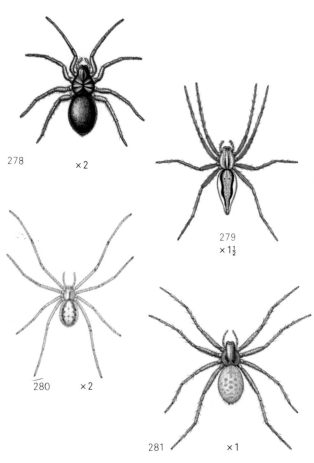

Female spiders: **278** Water Spider, *Argyroneta aquatica*.
279 Hunting Spider, *Pisaura mirabilis*. **280** *Enoplagnatha ovata*. **281** House Spider, *Tegenaria domestica*

175

Anatomy. The cephalothorax bears in front a number of simple eyes, their position and arrangement helping in classification. The chelicerae, the jaws or fangs, are stout, and contain the poison-glands from which ducts lead near to the tips of the sharp points. There is much difference in structure, according to species. To the cephalothorax are also attached the eight legs and a pair of palpi, or pedipalps. The palpi are remarkable appendages. In the female they are simple in construction, each ending in a claw. They help in feeling and compensate for the absence of antennae. In the male the palpi are complicated sex-organs, a male being easily recognizable by the swollen palpi (**282**). The female genitalia are situated in the lower surface and at the front of the abdomen, where the opening of the oviduct is. The aperture is called the *epigyne*. The method of pairing is unique in the animal

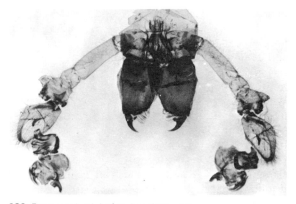

282 Fangs and palpi of male spider × 30

kingdom. The male's testis is at the base of the abdomen; the sperm is deposited by him on a specially constructed platform of silk, or he may dispense with this refinement. He then dips his palpi in the fluid and, thus charged, he transfers it to the female's epigyne for storing in reservoirs, called *spermathecae*, until required when eggs are laid. The sexual act is fraught with dangers for the male, as he is smaller than his mate, who will attack him and make a wedding breakfast of him, but often his smaller size and greater agility will save him. Spiders are, like insects, creatures guided by instinct. The persistent energy of insects would appear in spiders to be replaced by patience, which the scientist would no doubt prefer to term periods of inertia between immediate responses to external stimuli. At least that is so in respect of numerous species which lie in wait for victims; it does not at first appear quite so obvious in those which maraud in search of prey.

Spiders are fierce denizens of the undergrowth jungle. Many of their kind have invaded our houses, and even a strange unsuitable element, water, on the surface of which they carry on their relentless hunting. One, *Argyroneta aquatica* (**278**), the Water Spider, even goes into the water itself and lives there. They are always in pursuit of living prey, usually insects, so that spiders are praised because they are most active insect destroyers. It is pointed out that as every meal they make means the slaughter of a live and mostly pestilential creature, it follows that their activities are useful to man and the plants on which he depends for his existence.

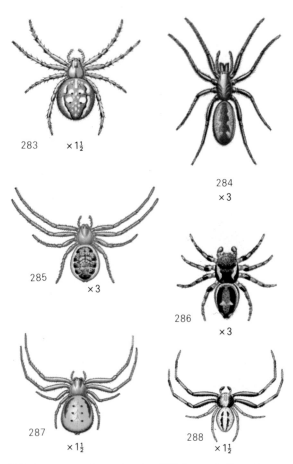

283 *Araneus quadratus*, female. **284** *Segestria florentina*, female. **285** *Diaea dorsata*, female. **286** *Evarcha falcata*, male. **287** *Misumena vatia*, female. **288** *M. vatia*, male

178

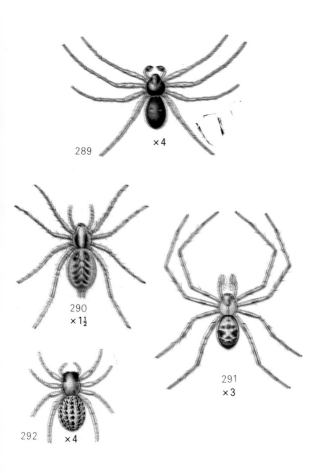

289 *Philodromus dispar*, male, **290** *Angelena labyrinthica*, female, **291** *Labulla thoracica*, male, **292** *Europhrys frontalis*, female

293 Hunting Spider, *Pisaura mirabilis,* female × 10

We are told to remember the old saying—

> If you wish to live and thrive,
> Let the spider run alive.

However, the zoologist will remark that this is counterbalanced by the fact that spiders attack all insects. They cannot be expected to discriminate conveniently for us between the allies and enemies of man, and the most that can be said in their favour is that they reduce the number of all insects. Spiders are actually of no economic importance. They neither harm man's possessions nor do they contribute in their activities anything of great value. Attempts have been made, it is true, to utilize the silk of spiders, but it is evident from experiments that on technical or economic grounds no industry could ever be created to rival in any way that which has been built up on the cocoon-spinning activities of silkworms (larvae of silk moths). Spiders are unique in their dependence on silk. It is used for making snares, for tying up victims whose struggles are likely to prove troublesome, for travelling—and even for 'flying', as well as for the cocoons to protect the eggs.

The female is an adept at finding suitable sites to lay her eggs, round which she then spins a protective mantle of silk. Some even go further than this: *Pisaura mirabilis* (**279**), a Hunting Spider, carries her cocoon about with her, so do the Wolf Spiders, *Lycosa*, rather sombre-coloured spiders, though the female goes one better to attract attention to her ways, for whilst she is hunting the young cling to her back.

Species that carry their cocoon about with them do so by having it attached to the jaws, or to the spinnerets. The spinnerets are the openings in the abdomen from which the silk emerges. The spider will offer violent resistance if we try to detach her precious possession. Smell seems to be the thing that attracts her to the cocoon, because if we take it away from her, and rub it on some light pellet, she will take this new object and carry it away, but not for long, as she soon becomes aware of the trickery and will start seeking her rightful property. Another mother will be found tearing her cocoon open to allow her offspring to escape. These species are thus doing their best in our eyes to retrieve the appalling reputation with which their kind is reproached.

Normally parental care ceases with the spinning

of the cocoon; some do not even go so far. If the female comes across her young she will not hesitate to make a meal of them. E. A. Robins, a well-known arachnologist, found that the young of *Amaurobius similis* (**276**) were actually eating their mother, who was still alive; experiments were repeated annually 'so it was not casual observance', as it happened again and again. This spider is the commonest and most widespread in these islands, and is usually found in cellars, sheds and the like. It is also one of our largest species, measuring 13 mm ($\frac{1}{2}$ in) long.

The number of eggs laid by spiders is often in the neighbourhood of eight hundred, the large number being required because the newly hatched spiderlings do not feed until after the first moult: life begins in a very earnest manner inside the silken home, for cannibalism breaks out, and it has been estimated that only about one hundred young spiders finally emerge.

When this happens they are miniatures of their parents. There is nothing that corresponds to the larval and pupal stages of insects. On the breaking of the cocoon the young are bent on dispersal, which some species effect by climbing on a fence, or other exposed position, and letting out strands of silk, or gossamer as it is called, in the breeze. When the spiderling finds that the wind gives sufficient pull it lets go, and so we have the remarkable feat of a flightless creature sailing through the air. Some observers maintain that spiders are able to control the length of gossamer, paying out more silk when the wind falls, and 'shortening sail' when it

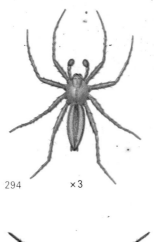

294 ×3

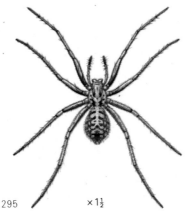

295 ×1½

294 *Micrommata virescens.* male. **295** *Tegenaria gigantea.*
female

183

increases. They naturally have to go where the wind takes them, often to an early doom. A classical example of this was furnished by Darwin, who in 1832, whilst on the Beagle, observed that the rigging of the vessel was suddenly invaded by numerous gossamer-borne spiders. The Beagle was some sixty miles from the nearest land. Since then cases have been recorded of much longer flights.

Most spiders do not spin webs, though they all make use of silk. When webs are made they differ according to the species of spider. The commonest house spider, *Tegenaria domestica* (**281**), makes the familiar untidy maze, whilst our large Garden Spider, *Araneus diadematus* (**275**) and *A. quadratus* (**283**), are makers of complex and beautiful webs. The spiders often vary in colour, especially the latter species.

Other common spiders are *Segestria senoculata* (**277**), which is widely distributed; it is often found wandering on walls, but these are more particularly the haunt of *Salticus scenicus* (**273**), the little Zebra Spider. *Diaea dorsata* (**285**), common in the South but not in the North, is one of our most beautiful species. It belongs to the family of Thomisidae, known as the Crab Spiders, as does *Misumena vatia* (female—**287**, male—**288**); the popular family name refers to the fact that they can run forwards, backwards or sideways. They do not spin webs, but lie in wait among vegetation, or in flowers, where they seize their victims. *M. vatia* even attacks bees; the spider may often be found when a bee is not seen to move away from a flower, which normally it leaves after a few seconds. It will be found held in the spider's fangs. Protective coloration, very evident in these spiders, is shown in one of the genus *Philodromus* (**289**).

Evarcha falcata (**286**) is very common everywhere, as also is *Euophrys frontalis* (**292**). Common in cellars, and in rooms at night is *Labulla thoracica* (**291**). It has quite handsome markings. Another species common in houses is *Tegenaria gigantea* (**295**). Also shown is a captive outdoor species, *Micrommata virescens* (**294**); it is a male, as shown by the abdomen. The female is entirely green.

INDEX

Figures in italic refer to the illustrations

186

189